I0084677

# CRYSTAL

## JUDY PARKINSON

crystal

# DEDICATION

*For Warren, John and Lisa*

# Also, by Judy Parkinson

*AN UNUSUAL ALLIANCE*

*MISSING IN RED*

# CHAPTER 1
## *Brett - 2022*

Although I had only known Crystal for a few weeks, my life changed forever the day she disappeared. Three years have passed and the sorrow and anger have gradually receded. But the memories are always there smouldering away in my subconscious. The depression that initially engulfed me clouded my days and there were times when I felt I would never see the sun. And then I met Eugene. With his help, I started clawing my way out. Life was still there for me to enjoy and I eventually faced each day with purpose.

Today had been good. I had organised delivery of my new textbook in time for the first university semester and was chuffed at the size of the order. This book was really bringing in the dough. I was just settling down with a beer in hand to watch the golf when my mobile phone rang. The voice on the other end was familiar. 'Brett? It's Danni.'

I felt a sharp sudden stab. I didn't hold grudges but I couldn't control the guardedness that crept into my voice. 'It's been a long time, Danni. What's up?'

'They've found Crystal, buried on a little island not far from where we anchored.'

I closed my eyes and felt my head go light. 'How do they know it's her?'

'I identified the bracelet.'

'Bracelet? What bracelet?'

'The one she was wearing on the last night.'

'Are you saying that a body has been confirmed as Crystal's, just by a bracelet? 'What about dental records, DNA?'

'They're checking that. Nothing's shown up so far. Brett, it has to be Crystal. The forensic people say the person died between two and four years ago. It was a woman between eighteen and thirty with a small frame, five-foot-seven tall.'

There was a short silence and Danni spoke again. 'The detective in charge says Crystal was murdered.' For a few seconds, my mind went blank. I had given up smoking years before—but longed to have one in my hand right now.

Danni's voice softened. 'No one knows when the body will be released. It could be ages. I felt we should do something for Crystal so I've organised a memorial service.'

'But you hardly knew her.'

'We knew her well enough. We were with her in her last days. She doesn't have anyone. Someone has to do something!

'What about Bradshaw?'

'Rick won't organise anything.'

'Who'll be at this memorial service?'

'Jaz, Steve, Rick, Shelly and us. You'll come, won't you?'

My mind started swirling. Seeing those people could plunge me back into depression. I couldn't risk it.

I particularly couldn't risk seeing Shelly again.

The past was buried and that's how I needed it to be. 'I'm sorry. I can't. And besides, I think it's ridiculous to have a memorial service when no one knows for sure it's Crystal.'

Danni's deep intake of breath was almost palpable. 'Brett, it *is* Crystal.'

'I'm busy, Danni. I can't manage the time.'

'You're lying.'

'Okay, I'm lying. I'm moving forward, not backward. I haven't seen Shelly in three years. How do you think I feel?'

'The police want to question all of us after the service. I don't know that you've got much choice. Next Saturday, two o'clock, the little park near the Akuna Bay Marina. Please, Brett.'

'I'll think about it.'

'How have you been?' she asked softly.

'Fine, and you?'

'Fine.' The line went quiet for ten seconds before Danni spoke again. 'Did you know Shelly got married?'

'No. Who?'

'A guy called Lance Gibson.'

My temples started to throb.

'I'm surprised you didn't know.'

'No, I didn't.' There was another silence. 'Goodbye, Danni.'

I put the phone in my pocket and went out onto

the deck. I leaned on the railing and closed my eyes. My other senses were immediately aroused. I heard the sea hurling itself against the rocks and I smelled the sharp, salty spray. After a moment or two, I opened my eyes. The great expanse of ocean stretched out before me its surface decorated with countless points of dancing sunlight. A cargo ship plodded its way across the horizon.

The old feelings of guilt started to prod me and I could feel myself falling back into the black hole that had imprisoned me for so long. I needed to stop falling, get back on track. I tried to employ the strategy that Eugene had taught me: *In times of stress, send away the unwelcome thoughts, concentrate on breathing, think of nature and other pleasant things.* I took a deep breath and gazed intently at the ocean. A cloud passed over the sun, and the sea suddenly changed from sapphire blue to a dull grey-green. The same cloud seemed to pass through my brain. *Control it Brett, concentrate.* I could feel a panic state approaching and I focused on the bush between my townhouse and the sea. But all I saw were countless clumps of bitou. The green leaves glistened and the bright yellow flowers swayed in the light breeze. I watched their smiling faces nodding their victory. They had been subjected to poison and fire, yet continued to flourish and multiply.

'Cursed bush,' I said aloud. I turned my attention from their mocking faces and slumped into a deck chair.

I resented this intrusion into my life and the resurrection of those memories. But they had never really gone away. I knew this day would eventually come. Even so, I wasn't ready for it. I had several reasons for not wanting to revisit the past. That time, three years ago, carried so much pain and so much guilt. Danni could talk about a body being found, but I could not be convinced that it was Crystal's. There were things I knew that others didn't.

As I sat there gazing at the sea, I accepted that I couldn't fight it any longer and I allowed the memories to flood in. I thought of that fateful boat trip and all the events leading up to it. I thought of Crystal and the first time I met her.

*

It was January 2019. Jaz had invited us over for a party to celebrate Steve's thirtieth birthday. My friendship with Steve went back to our university days. We first met when I was in my third year Engineering and Steve was doing his final year in Law. We lived in adjoining beach suburbs in Sydney's north and had spotted each other from time to time at sporting events. Recently we became members of the same golf club. Ours was an easy friendship. We both loved sport, beer and pretty girls.

Since graduating, Steve had done well for himself and had bought an attractive three-bedroom 'sixties' home on a big corner block in Warriewood. He had married Jacinta or Jaz as he called her, a year earlier. Although Jaz had different attitudes and interests from Steve, the marriage seemed to be working fine.

*

The party day came and it was hot and humid. Shelly was fussing in the bedroom. She had already changed her outfit twice and was now frowning at herself in the mirror.

'I've got nothing to wear.' Her mouth turned down at the corners. This usually meant fireworks and friction.

'That looks fine.' I muttered.

'It's crap.' She dragged the shirt off and headed back to the cupboard. I looked at my watch. 'We should have left ten minutes ago.' Shelly stubbornly ignored me and I sat through two more changes before we got away. By the time we were at Steve's place, more than a dozen people were gathered in the front garden. A tall hedge ran the entire front of the property providing privacy from the street. On the big expanse of lawn, tables and chairs were set up. The swimming pool sparkled invitingly at the southern end of the yard. Palms and other tropical trees added to the holiday atmosphere. Most of the other guests were strangers. I waved to the few I recognised.

We found Steve near the pool yakking with one of our golf club buddies. I had a box of booze tucked under my arm. I shook Steve's hand. 'You know Craig?' he asked.

'Sure do.' I shook Craig's hand. 'Where do you want these?' I indicated the beer.

'In the laundry, mate; there's a tub full of ice. Plonk 'em in and help yourself. Glasses are there, too.'

Steve kissed Shelly. 'You're looking gorgeous as usual.'

'Happy birthday Steve.' Shelly handed Steve a parcel. I had no idea what it might be. Shelly had a quirky sense of humour and nothing would surprise me. I didn't wait to find out and wandered around to the laundry. I deposited my beer in the tub, grabbed a cold one, and poured a glass of wine for Shelley

Back at the party, I found Shelly talking with Ban and Danni. Ben was an old schoolmate of Steve's and I'd met him and Danni a few years earlier. The two couples had married within a few months of each other.

Steve was into fitness and he and I played comp tennis every Tuesday night. We also played golf on Saturdays and worked out at the gym during the week. Steve had a barrel chest but not an ounce of fat on his body. He had a square jaw and regular features. His hair was starting to thin which made him look older than his thirty years. Ben, on the other hand, was battling a weight problem. He played a bit of golf but not much else. He had an addiction to sweet things and it wasn't unusual to see him demolishing a chocolate bar. He was two months older than Steve.

Although Danni and Jaz seemed poles apart in attitudes and tastes, they had become good mates. They were always friendly to Shelly yet somehow, I felt she hadn't quite made the grade with either of them.

Jaz was a bit of a 'New Age' disciple and dabbled in spiritualism, yoga and organic food. She usually wore 'way-out' gear. Today she had a scarf tied around her long, straight hair. Multiple beads hung around her flat chest and silver bangles clinked on her arms. Her colourful swirling skirt finished mid-calf revealing incredibly lofty shoes with numerous straps climbing up her legs. I always thought Jaz looked too skinny.

While Jaz was eccentric in her dress, Danni was fashionable and up-to-date. Today she wore designer white slacks and an expensive looking blue shirt. Danni had a pretty face and a bubbling personality—a real party girl. She wore her chestnut-coloured hair short and wavy.

Ben and I started discussing politics. Ben was on the other side of the fence but we both enjoyed a good argument. The humidity was intense and our usual good-natured sparring was becoming a bit loud and testy. I quickly finished my beer and pulled out of the fracas on the excuse of an empty can.

I wandered back to the laundry. A vaguely familiar-looking guy was hovering over the tub poking through the various bottles of wine. He straightened and grinned widely as I approached. 'Brett Carlton!' He walked towards me with arms outstretched. For a horrible moment, I thought he was going to kiss me.

He thrust out his hand. 'Mal Burton,' he effused as he wrung my hand with both of his. 'You probably don't remember me. We met here last year.' His small, intense eyes bored into me.

'I remember,' I lied. I selected a can at the top of the pile and pulled the tab.

'I've read your last book and it's incredibly good.'

My field in electronics had led me to write three technical books. These had all been taken up by the University of New South Wales and various technical colleges for their Electronics courses. It had been a good money-spinner but had brought no fame.

Hardly anyone outside the field knew I had written books. But this dude, he was treating me like a celebrity and it felt good to be acknowledged.

crystal

We talked, or rather he talked for fifteen minutes or more. By then, my beer was finished and I reached for another one. 'Better get back to the fray. My girl will think I've run out on her.'

I decided I needed to go to the loo and entered the house through the laundry. On the way back to the party, I took a shortcut to the front door. As I passed the main bedroom, I was surprised to see Shelly sitting at the bay window looking out onto the front garden. 'What are you doing in here?' I asked.

Shelly turned her shoulders towards me, her eyes still fixed on the activities outdoors. 'Can you believe it? Jaz is organizing egg-and-spoon races,' she groaned.

I peered through the window. More people had arrived and there were now at least twenty in the yard. Jaz was organising a group with eggs and spoons.

'They look like they're having fun.' I grinned.

'The last time I saw anything so silly was at a seventh birthday party.'

'You can't sit here all day.'

'I'm not going out into that circus, and I've had an empty glass for ages.' She thrust her glass at me.

I took the glass, took another look through the window, and moved off. I refilled the glass in the laundry and returned to the bedroom. I wordlessly handed it to her and wandered out into the yard. I was immediately assailed by Jaz.

'There you are, Brett. You're in the last heat. Where's Shelly?'

'Haven't a clue,' I lied.

I watched the next race with amusement. They certainly looked silly. Jaz came over and handed me an egg and spoon.

'Your turn,' she grinned. I felt a bit dopey but I'd had enough beer to give it a go. I put the spoon in my mouth, balanced an egg on top, and lined up with Steve and four other guys. Jaz blew a party horn and we all started running. It was harder than it looked, but I finished first, just beating Steve. We fell about laughing when Steve's egg fell off and splattered his good shoes.

Just then the front gate opened, and in walked an incredibly beautiful girl. She was tall and slim with long blonde hair. She wore white shorts which showed off her tanned legs. A little pink top emphasised her shapely breasts. Jaz welcomed her with a kiss on the cheek. 'Where's Rick?' she asked.

'He had to work. He'll be coming back around ten. Oh, there's the birthday boy,' the girl said, moving towards us. She handed Steve an ornately wrapped parcel which Steve accepted with a huge grin. He kissed the girl enthusiastically. She quickly pulled away from the kiss and turned her attention to me. Steve got the message and assumed the host role. 'Crystal, meet my good mate, Brett Carlton. Brett, this is the beautiful Crystal Morgan.'

'Hi, Brett.' Crystal's pretty mouth widened, creating dimples on either side. We looked into each other's eyes and there was a flash of electricity. Neither of us noticed Steve moving off.

'Can I get you a drink?' I asked.

'Please, white wine would be lovely.'

I was relieved to see a full bottle and some glasses on the nearby table. That meant I didn't have to go traipsing back to the laundry. I handed her the drink. She smiled her thanks through wide blue eyes and took a tiny sip before asking, 'Are you a close friend of Steve's?'

'Pretty close.'  Just then I saw Shelly walking toward us.

'Thank God that stupid game's all over and we can be grown-ups again,' she muttered.

'Shelly, meet Crystal,' I said.  Shelly seemed to notice Crystal for the first time. 'Crystal, this is Shelly.'

Crystal smiled. 'Hi,' she offered her hand.  I was taken aback by Shelly.  She eyed Crystal with a stony face and shook her hand silently.  I thought she was bloody rude.

The day wore on and Steve started the barbeque around seven.  As it was mid-summer, it was still light. Fairy lights had been strung up between two big palm trees.  The guests were seated at three long tables.

I was sitting next to Crystal—by chance or design, I wasn't sure.  But it felt good to be so close to her.  She had her back to me and was talking to Ben on her other side.  I was totally immersed in her hair—the golden streaks and the soft, cascading waves. I smelled the citrus fragrance and was in a sort of spell.

Then the spell was broken by a force coming from—where?  I looked away from the hair and to the source of the force, straight across the table into Shelly's cold and cutting eyes.

I raised my eyebrows as if to say '*What?*'
and then Crystal turned her head and I was drawn from one pair of eyes to another. 'Sorry to have my back to you, Brett,' she said. She turned her body towards me

and leaned on her elbows.

That's okay,' I smiled.

.       'I was just having a nice chat with Ben.   He went to school with Steve. That's such a long friendship.  So special, I envy them.'

'And you, how did you meet Jaz and Steve?' I asked.

'Jaz and I work together.   I haven't known her for long but already she's a good friend.'

'All you people that want your steak still alive, come and get it,' called Steve from the barbeque.

'How do you like yours?' I asked Crystal.

'Not still alive,' she smiled.

Shelly came over and thrust an empty plate under my nose.  'You like your steak rare. It's ready,' she hissed.  I gave Crystal a little shrug and followed Shelly to the barbeque.

'Here's a nice bloody one for you, mate.' Steve shovelled an enormous steak onto my plate.  'And here's a medium rare for Shelly.' He delicately placed a smaller steak on her waiting plate.  'Salads and bread are on the table. Help yourselves.'  Steve turned his attention to the next guest.  Shelly and I walked to the table and served ourselves from the assortment of salads.

Without looking at me, Shelly whispered, 'Come and sit with me. Leave the little bimbo alone.'

'For  Christ's  sake,'  I  muttered.    I  couldn't understand her vitriol.

We  ate  our  meal  in  silence.   I  noticed  that someone else had taken my seat next to Crystal and they were in earnest conversation. My good mood had been destroyed and I compensated myself by pouring a big glass of red wine. Steve put on some music and couples started dancing.

The sun finally slipped away and darkness fell. I had trouble keeping my eyes off Crystal. She was now dancing with Ben.

Around nine, Jaz came out of the house carrying an enormous cake. It was shaped like a tennis racket and covered in chocolate icing.

She tapped a glass with a spoon to get attention. 'Thank you all for helping Steve celebrate his thirtieth birthday. If the old fart eats this cake I made, it will probably be his last cake—and birthday.' There was a general chuckle as Jaz lit the candles. Unsteadily, Steve got to his feet and blew hard at the candles. Three remained alight. He blew again. It occurred to me, in my alcoholic haze, how unhygienic this custom is. The birthday cake would now be awash with all of Steve's germs and I decided not to have any.

We all sang 'Happy Birthday'. Steve gave a silly speech. People chuckled. Ben got up and gave an even sillier one. I looked at Shelly and winked. 'There'll be a couple of sore heads tomorrow.'

'I wouldn't want your head on my shoulders tomorrow either,' she said, focusing on the glass in my hand.

'I'm okay. Want to dance?' I asked.

Steve changed the disc and turned up the volume. Shelly and I shuffled around on the tiled deck.

After a few minutes, she pulled away and walked over to Steve and Danni. I was cornered again by my book fan whose name I couldn't remember. The night wore on and people started drifting off.

It was nearly eleven when the front gate opened

and a man entered. I heard Crystal say, 'Here's Rick.'

As the guy approached, I noted he was about fifty, had a bit of a paunch hanging over his belt, and was of average height. His sparse grey hair matched his moustache, his face was lined, and his lips were tight and thin.

He talked for a while with Steve and then sat next to Crystal at the table. Crystal seemed really happy to see him. She snuggled up to him and put her hand on his. I couldn't work out the attraction. She was so beautiful and he was so old and ordinary.

'Rick, this is Brett,' said Crystal. I stretched my arm across the table and we shook hands.

'Not much fun having to work on a Saturday night, mate,' I grinned.

'I don't *have* to work Saturdays,' he said sourly. I caught Crystal's expression. She looked a little tense.

'What do you do?' asked Shelly.

'I'm helping a mate out,' he said stiffly.

'Doing?' asked Shelly. I was surprised at her persistence. Obviously, the guy didn't want to talk about himself.

'Night watching,' he muttered, taking a gulp of his beer.

Then Crystal broke in. 'Rick works in advertising during the week.'

'Where do you live, Crystal?' asked Danni.

'Rick and I live in Mona Vale,' she smiled up at Rick as she spoke. So, they lived together! What in hell's name did she see in him?

By midnight everyone was gone except us, Ben, Danni, Crystal and Rick. I had had quite a bit to drink, and decided that if Shelly was too sloshed to drive, we could get a cab home.

I poured myself another red wine.

Steve came over and pulled Shelly up for a dance. Rick was talking with Ben and Crystal was at the drinks table pouring some water. I wandered over.
'Hi, like to dance?'

'Sure.' She smiled and I took her hand. We moved to the music which was slow and sensual. Crystal's body seemed to melt into mine and I wanted the dance to last forever. Shelly and Steve had stopped dancing and seemed to be in deep conversation. The tune finished and Crystal gently pulled away. I followed her back to the table. Rick, Danni, Dave and Jaz were sharing a joke. Steve and Shelly wandered over. Steve was grinning broadly. 'Shelly has come up with a great idea. Tell 'em, Shell.'

'I thought it might be fun to hire a cruiser on the long weekend—take a run up the Hawkesbury.'

'Sounds good,' said Jaz.

'I'll be in that,' said Danni.

I wondered why Shelly hadn't said anything to me but I made no comment.

'I'll look into it,' said Shelly.

'We'll need an eight-berth,' said Danni. Shelly frowned. 'Six will do. There are only six of us.'

'What about Crystal and Rick? You'd like to come, wouldn't you, Crystal?' Danni asked with raised eyebrows.

I noticed Shelly's frown deepen. Before Crystal could answer, Shelly spoke.

'We could never get an eight-berth at this late stage. It's less than two weeks away.'

I looked at Crystal. A little cloud had come over her lovely face. I thought again that Shelly was being rude.

'We've got a friend who owns an eight-berth cruiser. If he's not using it himself, I'm sure he'd hire it out to us. I'll call him tomorrow,' offered Jaz.

I caught Shelly's expression. Her mouth was tight and her eyes were glaring. We left the party soon after. Shelly took the wheel and drove with a stern face. 'You weren't very nice to Crystal,' I said.

'What do you mean?'

'You were excluding her from the boat trip, right in front of her. You didn't care that she might be hurt.'

'For Christ's sake, we don't know those people. We only met them tonight.' Shelly's jaw was set hard and she nearly side-swiped a parked car. I thought I should shut up if I didn't want an accident.

She drove into the downstairs garage, parked the car roughly, walked to the lift, and closed it in my face. I took the stairs and while climbing them, started puzzling over our relationship.

Shelly had a bad temper and there was a side to her that I could never figure.

*

I first met Shelly in early 2018. I'd arranged to meet Ben at the club for a drink after work. He was fifteen minutes late but swaggered in as if nothing was amiss. I decided to say nothing and greeted him with a grin and a handshake. 'I'm surprised you're allowed out,'

I said taking a swig of my beer.

'Got to set the rules right from the start, mate,' he smirked. 'What's happened to *your* little number?'

'Kylie?  Oh, we've had a parting of the ways. She was getting a bit demanding, started talking about weddings and babies.'

'Marriage ain't all that bad.'

'I'm not ready for it.  Anyway, Kylie had a few missing links,' I said taking another swig.

We talked sport and politics.  All the while, I'd been noticing an attractive girl sitting alone in the booth across the way.

'She looks a bit lonely,' I winked at Ben.

'Go for it, mate.'

I wandered over.  'Like some company?'

'I'm waiting for someone.  Looks like he's not coming,' she sighed.

'Brett Carlton.' I held out my hand.

'Shelly Lawson.'

'Join us.'

Soon after, Ben drifted off and Shelly and I had another drink.

An hour later, Shelly glanced at the empty booth. 'He's definitely not coming,' she said quietly.

'A foolish man.  Who is he anyway?'

'Just a business acquaintance.'

'Not a boyfriend?'

Shelly shook her head and took a sip of her wine.

'Do you have a boyfriend?'

'Not at present.  Do you have a girlfriend?'

'Not at present,' I grinned.  I looked at my watch.

'It's gone seven. Would you like dinner?'

'That would be nice.'

The golf club had a pleasant dining room and served good food. I ordered a bottle of wine and we looked at the menu. Shelly chose the baked lamb and I had the surf and turf.

'Do you work?' I asked.

'Of course, doesn't everyone?'

'Not everyone. What do you do?'

'Not very exciting, I'm with a hire car company, at the Cross. I work in their accounts department. And you?'

'I lecture at the University of New South Wales—electronics.'

'How impressive!'

'It's a living.' I tried to sound modest but I was aware that university lecturing carried a certain amount of status.

We finished our meal and said goodbye at our respective cars. I took her phone number and she took mine.

The next night she phoned me. 'Brett, I want to thank you again for last night.'

'You're very welcome. I enjoyed it.'

'Can I take you to my favourite restaurant this weekend?'

'I'd like to see you again, Shelly, but there's no need for you to feel you owe me anything.'

'I insist. How about Saturday?'

'Saturday's fine.'

'Only one condition, you have to pick me up and

take me home.'

'Of course.' She gave me her address.

The following Saturday night Shelly welcomed me into her small apartment in Kings Cross. She was wearing a classic black dress which showed off her lean, trim figure. A short string of pearls gleamed at her throat. A matching clasp secured her silky blonde hair which was pulled back and piled on top of her head. Her high-heeled sandals brought her face level with mine. I was six-two and I guessed Shelly was around five-ten without the heels.

'We can walk there.' she said, steering me through the doorway.

Five minutes later, we entered the restaurant. I was immediately enveloped in its delightful ambience. The soft music, fresh flowers, glittering silver and delightful food aromas, all set the stage for a great meal.

I relaxed easily with Shelly. She was a lot smarter than Kylie and I enjoyed her repartee. I learned that she was a 'fitness freak' and worked out every day. Well, we had that in common!

We ordered a second bottle of wine. She told me about her family. Her father had run out on her mother when she was a toddler, and her mother had died soon after.

'How did you get on?'

'An auntie took me in and I stayed with her until I was eighteen. Then she died too. But I was able to look after myself by then.'

'I guess I've been really lucky. My folks are still alive and healthy and I've got a kid sister. I've never had any big hiccups in my life—so far.'

The small three-piece band started playing a romantic tune. Shelly widened her eyes and put her head to one side. 'Let's dance,' she said. I held her close and we shuffled around on the tiny dance floor. The wine was going to my head, or was it her perfume?

We finished our second bottle and Shelly reached across the table and took my hand. 'Let's go home,' she whispered.

In her apartment, Shelly threw off her black dress and almost tore my clothes off. She straddled me on the bed and dominated the action. I had never experienced anything quite like this before. But I was happy to lie back and just enjoy it. She was strong and muscular and took control. She knew what to do and how to do it. I came before she did but this didn't worry her.

The night was young and she had me going again in no time. But this time I took charge. Eventually, we both fell asleep.

I awoke the next morning to the aroma of coffee.

Shelly approached the bed carrying two steaming cups. She was wearing a loose see-through top. She handed me the coffee and sat on the edge of the bed.

'Sleep well?' she smiled over the top of her cup.

'Never better.'

A few weeks later Shelly moved into my apartment. We often got together with Steve, Jaz, Ben and Danni for barbeques and drinks. Shelly liked the camaraderie.

But it wasn't long before I discovered a chink in

Shelly's armour. She had been complaining to me
about the inefficiencies and problems with the
hire car company. She decided to prepare a 'Fact and
Proposal' document and worked studiously on her
project for three nights. On the third night, she
emerged from the study all smiles. 'It's done and I'll be
handing it to the CEO tomorrow. If this doesn't get me
a salary rise, nothing will.'

'Well done,' I winked at her with a grin.

The next day she came home from work all
bright and chirpy. 'How was your day?' she asked.

I was making a salad. 'Not bad. I finished all my
lectures before three and took an early mark.' I poured
her a drink and started the barbeque. I usually
prepared all the meals. Shelly hated cooking and I
quite liked it. The night was warm and balmy and I had
set the table on the deck. We sat down for our meal.
The steak was perfect. I was really enjoying it when I
noticed that Shelly had gone quiet and wasn't eating.

'What's wrong? Is the steak too rare?'

'Fuck your steak.' She pushed the plate away
and stood. 'You show no interest in anything I
do. All you think about is yourself.'

'What do you mean?'

'What do I *mean?*' she screeched. 'I have just
re-written the books for the fucking Grossett Hire Car
Company and you don't give a shit.' She threw her
serviette on the table, nearly knocked over the chair,
and stormed off to the bedroom.

She didn't speak to me for four days. After that,
I trod very carefully. I always made sure I praised her

for even the most minor achievement, but the more
I encouraged her, the more she bragged.

But then I had another slip-up. It was a Saturday
six months later. I'd had a great day at golf and ran
second in the comp. It was just after five when I got
home. Shelly was in the kitchen. 'Like a coffee?' she
asked.

'Thanks,' I said, grabbing the paper. A short
while later, Shelly handed me a cup of coffee and
placed a cake on the coffee table. 'Like a piece?'

'Thanks,' I said absently.
She cut off a slice of cake and handed it to me on a
plate. I ate it, drank the coffee, and continued reading.

'Didn't you like it?' she said quietly.

'What?'

'The cake—you didn't like it!' Her voice had
risen.

'I ate it, didn't I?'

'But you didn't say anything. That tells me you
didn't like it. Well, if you didn't like it, you can fucking
wear it.' Her aim was good and my face was covered
in cake and cream.

It didn't occur to me for a second that she had
made the cake. Shelly hadn't made a single dinner in
the time we had been together. A cake was the last
thing I had expected. Without a word, I went to the
bathroom, washed my face, and drove back to the golf
club.

\*

Towards the end of the year, I was thinking
seriously of giving up my tutoring job. I was making good

money from my books which were in demand at the beginning of each year.

Updating them annually took time and effort, and I was starting to feel pressured.  I decided to quit the full-time tutoring job and just look for part-time lecturing.

I talked to Shelly about my decision.  She flew into a rage.

'How do you think we can ever get anywhere if you don't work?' she shouted.

'I'm getting good royalties from my books and I'm working on a new one right now.'

'We'll always live in an apartment and drive cheap cars.  Don't you have any ambition?'  she grizzled.

'If you don't like it, you know what you can do.'  I felt angry and irritated.   The subject was never raised again but soon after, she started coming home late, two or three nights every week.

'What's going on?' I asked.

'We need the money.  I'm doing extra shifts,' she snapped.  I felt then that our relationship was thinning out.

# CHAPTER 2
## *Brett*

Two days after Steve's party, Jaz phoned to say she had booked an eight-berth cruiser for three nights starting Friday, the 24th of January. Arrangements were made to meet beforehand to sort out the food and drinks for the trip.

We met at Steve's place the following Saturday afternoon. From the start, there was friction. Ben was writing the grog list and mumbled something about four bottles of bourbon.

'Why would you want four bottles?' I asked.

'We'll get through it.' Ben turned to Rick. 'You like a drop, don't you, Rick?'

'Never touch the stuff,' growled Rick.

'Two bottles are plenty,' I said. Ben grudgingly changed the number. I got my way with the beer too. I argued that all the guys drank beer and we needed at least four cases. There were raised voices coming from the next room and I guessed the girls were having their disagreements as well.

On the way home, Shelly filled me in.

'You'll never guess what happened. Danni wanted to buy six kilos of prawns. Can you imagine trying to keep them fresh? There's bugger-all refrigeration on these boats. It'll be a miracle if the milk doesn't go off.'

'It'll be a miracle if we're still friends at the end,' I said cynically.

*

The departure day soon came. We arrived at the Akuna Bay Marina promptly at six. Steve and Jaz were in the office collecting the keys. I grabbed a trolley, returned to the car, and started offloading the boxes of grog. During this time Rick's car pulled into the space alongside. Crystal called through the open window. 'What gorgeous weather! Aren't we lucky!'

'Sure are. See you on board, jetty 14.' I moved off pushing the heavy, precariously-loaded trolley.

Eventually, we were all aboard. 'It's lovely,' said Crystal.

'Yes. It's a nice boat,' agreed Jaz.

The boat was a pleasant surprise. The back deck had seating on both sides and a set of steps led up to the flight deck. The main cabin had a long lounge chair on each side. Further on, a curving lounge encircled a table. Two steps down were the galley on the starboard side and the bathroom on the port side. Another two steps down were two curtained cabins divided by a thin partition. Each had a double bed.

'Who brought that case?' Steve pointed to a gigantic suitcase sitting on the table.

'It's mine,' said Danni.

'Well, it can't stay. There's no room. You'll have to take it back to your car.'

I was surprised by the sharpness in Steve's voice.

'My clothes are in it,' Danni protested.

'You'll have to put them in plastic bags like the rest of us. You only need some undies and a couple of tees.'

Danni looked mournfully at Jaz. 'There's nowhere to put it, lovey,' said Jaz. Shelly and I were keeping out of it and busied ourselves putting away the beer and wine. We had both noted Steve's instructions on what to bring and had stuffed our gear into plastic bags. I had packed three pairs of jocks, two T-shirts, two pairs of shorts, a windcheater, a towel and my boardies. Shelly had brought similar things plus a colourful caftan she had just finished making.

'Where do I get plastic bags?' muttered Danni. Jaz hunted through the cupboards. 'Here are some kitchen-tidy bags.' She handed a roll to Danni.

Danni, pouting, upended the suitcase and started stuffing things into the bags. She grabbed the case and went ashore leaving three brimming bags on the table. Steve looked painfully at them but said nothing.

We all busied ourselves putting stuff away. Five minutes later Danni returned.

'Let's get the show on the road,' muttered Ben.

'Like me to drive?' I offered.

'I'm the captain, matey,' said Ben, climbing the steps to the flight deck.

I followed him up and was amused to see him put on a captain's hat. Within minutes the boat was in motion and we steered out of the marina.

crystal

The early evening was warm, and we sat on the deck.  Steve brought out an esky full of ice and drinks.

'Champagne, girls?'

'Yes, please!' said Danni.

It wasn't long before we all had a drink in our hands.  Rick and I were drinking beer, and Steve and Ben were drinking stiff bourbons and cokes.  After an hour, I went up to the wheel and stood beside Ben as he steered the boat through the still green water.

'Like me to take over?' I offered.

'No, thanks.  But you can get me a refill.'  He put his three middle fingers together indicating the 'nip' size.

'Where are we heading?'

'White Island.  It's not far from the mainland and the anchorage is pretty safe.'

I started feeling irritated by Ben.  The captain's hat wasn't a joke.  I thought he was starting to act like a controlling smart-arse.  I got his drink and grabbed myself another beer.

As we motored, the sun sank behind the passing hills.  A full moon rose, casting silver shafts on the water.  The breeze was light and the night was soft and balmy.

We dropped anchor after two hours of easy cruising.

Jaz had set up some CDs and the music was creating a lazy, romantic atmosphere.

I had trouble keeping my eyes away from Crystal.  She was the most beautiful girl I'd ever seen.  I still wondered what she saw in Rick.

The girls put together a cold meat and salad dinner and we ate on the deck.

'What are the sleeping arrangements?' asked Shelly.

'As you know, there are two double cabins. The side lounges turn into two singles and the table converts to a double,' said Jaz.

'Who gets what?' asked Danni.

'We'll draw to see who gets what,' said Jaz.

'I think we should rotate each night, to be fair,' said Danni.

'I agree.' Jaz disappeared into the cabin and returned a few minutes later with a plastic bag. 'I've put the draw in here.' She held up the bag to Danni.

Danni drew out a piece of paper. Her face lit up. 'Goody, we've got a cabin.'

'Now you, Shelly.'

Shelly cautiously withdrew a paper. 'We've got a cabin, too.' She sighed with relief.

I felt grateful as the side sofas looked decidedly skinny and I couldn't imagine a good sleep there. Crystal and Rick drew the sofas and Jaz and Steve got the table.

'We'll all have something different tomorrow,' said Jaz. She turned up the music. 'Let's dance!' she shouted.

I shuffled around with Shelly. Ben and Danni joined in. Steve then grabbed Shelly and I saw Jaz pull up Rick.

I walked to Crystal and held out my hand. She moved towards me. Then she was in my arms. I breathed in her fragrance and bent my head so that my cheek touched hers. She drew her body even closer to mine and we moved slowly to the rhythm of the music.

Her soft warm body was sending sparks of arousal through me and I wanted the moment to last forever. But the spell was broken by Rick who came up behind and roughly tapped me on the shoulder. He had left Jaz standing alone embarrassed and abandoned. I had no option but to give Crystal to Rick and dance with Jaz.

We shuffled around the deck for a minute or two and then Jaz whispered in my ear. 'Be careful, Brett.'

'What do you mean?'

'Rick is jealous and possessive. I've noticed the way you look at Crystal—and so has Rick!'

I said nothing and we continued dancing. Jaz whispered again. 'She attracts men like bees to honey.'

'That's understandable,' I said.

'At the office Christmas party, we invited staff from the North Sydney office. We also invited some clients. They were all dotty over Crystal,' whispered Jaz.

'And how did Crystal respond—to the dottiness?'

'She seemed totally unaware.'

'Well then, if Crystal is unaware, Rick's got nothing to worry about.' The music stopped and Jaz moved away to change the CD.

The night wore on, as did our drinking.

Steve had just handed out the punch line of a dirty joke when Crystal pulled a book from her bag. A pen was clipped onto its luminous pink faux-leather cover. She moved to the corner lounge and started writing.

'What are you doing, Crystal?' Danni asked.

'Oh, it's just my diary. I write in it every night. I've been doing it since...forever.'

'What do you write?' I asked.

'Everything that happened during the day. It's a habit I can't seem to break.' She smiled as she resumed her writing.

Around midnight Danni announced she was off to bed. She and Ben disappeared behind their curtain.

'I'm off, too,' said Shelly, walking to our allocated cabin. She pulled the curtain shut. I wasn't ready for bed and sat with the others on the deck. Crystal made coffee and we all sat quietly drinking.

'What an enormous moon.' Crystal gazed heavenward. It did seem enormous. Its brightness illuminated the river in all directions.

'It'll be good weather tomorrow, judging by the sky,' said Steve. I looked at the canopy above. Countless stars glittered in the cloudless expanse. Yes indeed, tomorrow should be just fine.

I fell into bed around one o'clock and was soon off to sleep. Sex was not an option as we were all so close.

I awoke with a start. I looked at the illuminated dial of my watch which said it was three o'clock.

Then I became tuned into a cacophony of sleeping sounds. They seemed to be coming from all over the boat. A curtain covered the porthole at my shoulder. I pulled it aside and peered out. The moonlight was still strong, almost like day. I could see a big cruiser anchored some distance away.

I fell back onto my pillow, closed my eyes, and drifted into a deep sleep.

I awoke soon after dawn. Shelly was sleeping soundly. I moved quietly through the main cabin and out onto the deck. The sun was still low in the sky but already I could feel the heat radiating from it. I leaned on the railing and looked across to the island that had been in darkness when we arrived last night. A fringe of white sand curled around thick bush intermingled with tropical trees. It looked peaceful and beckoning. The big cruiser was nowhere in sight.

Feeling a bit seedy from last night's beer, I decided on a swim. I went back to the cabin and pulled on my boardies. Everyone seemed to be still sleeping.

The water was cold. Visibility was poor and I didn't stay in long. Stories of sharks and fatal encounters prompted an early exit. When I climbed back on board I was surprised and pleased to see Crystal on the deck.

The rays from the rising sun played on her hair, creating a halo effect. She handed me a towel. 'Thanks,' I said as I rubbed it over my dripping body. She put her hands on my chest. 'Nice,' she said. She was wearing a bikini under her sheer top. I put my hand on her breast. It was warm and firm. 'Nice,' I said.

Just then Rick appeared at the top of the stairs. I quickly withdrew my hand. Rick flicked his cigarette butt overboard, threw me a filthy look, and turned back inside.

The rest of the group arose one by one. I was astounded to see Danni appearing in what looked like a head full of torture instruments. 'What's that in your hair?' I asked with raised brows.

'I've got straight hair and if I don't put it in rollers, I look like the witch from hell,' she wailed.

I noticed with amusement that she was wearing

a nightie. The rest of us had fallen into bed in our clothes from the day before.

It wasn't long before there was a line to the shower. We had our breakfasts in a disorderly fashion and no one seemed particularly bright. But the weather was magnificent and we decided to spend the day on the island.

After two dinghy trips, we were all ashore along with our supplies for lunch. Steve and Ben set about finding timber for a barbeque. I started organising the 'bar'. Jaz was doing some stretching and posing on the sand.

'Is that yoga?' I asked.

'It is, and I think you could all do with a bit of stretching and meditation after what some of you consumed last night.'

Within a few minutes, Jaz had us all lined up. She demonstrated a pose and encouraged us to copy. It was harder than it looked. She went through a few more poses.

I couldn't see the point in the exercise and felt a good swim and a run would be far more beneficial. I was glad when it was all over.

Steve started building a barbeque and I wandered into the bush looking for more wood. There was plenty lying around. I returned with an armful and threw it onto the growing pile. Danni was carefully placing thin sticks along the beach.

'What are you up to?' I asked.

'I thought it would be fun if we had a game of 'fly.'

'What's fly?' asked Crystal.

crystal

Danni gave a demonstration and everyone agreed to join in.

'The girls were first to compete.  Shelly was the strongest and most athletic.  Her long muscular legs made the broad jumps look easy.  She won the girls' competition in record time.  I didn't have any trouble beating Steve and Ben, but Rick was hanging in close.  I was surprised by his agility.  His age and his paunch had deceived me and he seemed hell-bent on beating me. As we competed, the sticks were moved further apart and our broad jumps were getting more difficult.  I saw the look of determination in Rick's eyes and my competitive spirit rose.  The last jump was difficult.  I gave it all I had and cleared the stick. Rick didn't make it.  He walked off without a word, slumped onto the sand, and picked up his book.

After the game, the grog came out, and around midday, Steve lit the barbeque.  The girls made up some salads and we were soon eating lunch.

I found a smooth rock to sit on.  Crystal and Rick were sitting next to each other on the sandy slope which rose up from the beach.

A gentle warm breeze was moving through the trees and the sun was shining brilliantly in an intensely blue sky. I looked at Crystal and was suddenly overcome with a feeling of pure happiness. I had read somewhere that it is rare to experience this type of joy. The last time I remembered having it was ten years before.  I had just finished my final school exams.  My two best mates had organised a hike down the south coast.  We were walking through a beautiful rainforest when I was overcome with this incredible insouciance.

Now I was feeling it again. But it wasn't only the ambience of my surroundings that was responsible. It was Crystal. I felt so close to her. It was as if she was tied up with my future and part of my destiny. I felt she might be my 'forever' girl. I looked away and saw Jaz watching me. She shook her head slowly. Jaz didn't miss a thing.

The island was small, and I decided to explore.

'Anyone feels like a walk?' I invited.

'Later,' said Steve.

No one else replied so I took off by myself. It was a pretty island. Native birds were everywhere and I even spotted some small marsupials. I completed the full circumference in less than forty minutes.

When I returned, I found most of the others stretched out on the sand, sun baking and sleeping—all but Crystal. She was at the far end of the beach, a little up the hill, with her back turned.

As I approached, I saw she was talking on her mobile. She quickly finished her conversation when she saw me coming.

'How was your walk?' she asked.

'Short but sweet. You should have come.'

'Yes. I could do with the exercise.'

'I don't mind doing it again,' I said. She smiled widely. Then her smile slowly faded as she looked beyond me. I turned and saw Rick approaching.

'Let's see the island, Crystal,' he said.

She gave me a tiny shrug and walked to Rick.

We returned to the boat around six and there was

another line for the shower. We had nibbles and drinks on the deck. When darkness fell, a breeze came up and we decided to go inside.

'Anyone bring a pack of cards?' asked Danni.

'There's a pack in that cupboard,' said Jaz.

We started poker and before long, it turned into 'Strip Jack Naked.' It was hilarious. As I only had on a pair of shorts, my jocks and my watch, it wasn't long before I was starkers. Most of the others were sparsely dressed and soon they were all down to their undies. Rick had left the game the moment it stopped being regular poker. He walked out onto the deck with an expression of contempt.

I was aroused by the sight of Crystal's beautiful body. Shelly caught me looking and gave me a cold, hard stare. Rick came back to get himself another beer. His expression was livid when he saw Crystal's bare top.

'Ready for bed, Crystal?' he shouted.

Crystal's face shadowed. She looked like a little kid being found out doing something naughty.

'Coming, Rick.' She got up in the middle of a hand and headed for their allotted cabin. This put the mockers on the game and we wound it up soon after.

As bad luck would have it, Shelly and I scored the table. I slept fitfully and woke around two. I determined that it must be the snoring that was disturbing my sleep, Steve and Ben being the main culprits.

I got up and went out onto the deck. Crystal was leaning against the railing looking out. In the distance, I saw a big cruiser. It looked exactly like the one I'd seen the night before. I stood beside Crystal.

'Hi.' she said softly.

'I saw that boat last night,' I said.

Crystal said nothing but turned and kissed me softly. 'Goodnight, Brett.' She walked back inside. I decided to take a closer look at the boat and climbed up to the flight deck. Finding the binoculars, I zoomed in on the cruiser. It was big. I estimated at least sixty-five feet. It was sleek and modern and glowed in the strong moonlight. I watched it for a while and then returned to my 'bed' and fell into a deep sleep.

The next morning Ben was up bright-eyed and bushy-tailed. He had us all organised by ten and ordered Steve to lift the anchor.

'Where today, captain?' asked Steve.

'Dead Man's Island,' said our self-appointed commander, as he climbed to the flight deck.

My irritation re-ignited. None of us had been invited to give input into where we would spend the weekend but 'Captain Bligh' had taken control again.

I climbed the stairs to the flight deck and stood quietly next to Ben. The boat travelled at a steady speed churning up the dull green water.

After a while, I broke the silence. 'What makes you think we all want to go to Dead Man's Island?'

'Why wouldn't you?'

'I don't know anything about it. For all I know, there could be better places.'

'That's just it. You don't know. You forget I used to own a boat. I know this river like the back of my hand. For the limited time we've got, this is the best place. Trust me.'

I left him, feeling mixed emotions. In the main cabin, there was something going on. Shelly was banging on the shower room door. 'For God's sake, Danni, how much longer are you going to be? I need to go to the loo.'

A few seconds later, the door opened and Danni came out clutching a bag brimming with her hair rollers.

'Don't tell me you've been doing your hair!' Shelly screeched.

'It's the only mirror on board,' pleaded Danni.

'For Christ's sake!' muttered Shelly pushing past Danni and slamming the door closed behind her.

Around eleven, the grog came out. Crystal, Jaz and Shelly were sticking to soda. Danni was keeping up with us guys.

I started thinking about what Ben had said and felt remorseful for my comments. I climbed up to the flight deck. 'Look, Ben, I've been thinking. You're doing a good job organising this jaunt. I was out of turn before, sorry.'

'Forget it, mate.' We shook hands. I cuffed him playfully on the shoulder. We stood comfortably in silence.

'Dead Man's Island,' said Ben looking ahead. A mass of land covered in tropical trees and shrubs loomed up ahead. We dropped anchor in deep water a short distance from the shore. We set up a barbeque on the sand and within an hour we were eating. There was talk of taking a walk around the island. But the map told us this island was much bigger than White Island and probably not so easy to circumnavigate. I wandered down to the water and dived in. It was fresh and invigorating. Shelly, Danni and Steve joined me. I looked up and saw Crystal paddling near the shore.

'Come on in,' I called

She shook her head. 'I can't swim.'

I swam over to her and splashed her playfully. Shelly surfaced in front of me and splashed me hard in the face. She wasn't smiling.

After the swim, people started flopping down on towels. Rick and Steve seemed to be asleep and Ben was reading a book. Jaz and Danni were lying flat on their backs talking softly together and Shelly was standing at the water's edge. Crystal seemed to have disappeared.

With all the eating and drinking, I was feeling stodgy and needed to exercise. Back home, my usual daily routine included a run at lunchtime plus at least one hour in the gym. I decided to 'do' the island and took the narrow track at the left end of the beach.

It wound its way through thick scrubby bush and gradually inclined upwards. The sand was soft and deep.

After thirty minutes or so, I reached a plateau. I was surprised to see Crystal standing near the edge. She had her back to me but I could tell she was talking on her mobile. As I approached her, I heard her say something that sounded like: *'I'll call you as soon as I know. Don't worry. I'll be okay.'* When she saw me, she looked a bit flustered and put her phone back in the pocket of her flimsy shirt. 'Brett!'

'Hey, what are you doing up here?' I asked.

'Just walking and looking. Did you see the

graves?' She moved over to a small area surrounded by a hedge. I followed her. There were three graves, all with headstones. The earth on top of each grave was covered with soft mossy grass.

'They died here ninety years ago—shipwrecked,' said Crystal.

I read the headstones. It appeared the three were members of the same family; a man, his wife and their daughter. A glass-covered photo was attached by rusty clips to the centre grave. A gaunt-faced man stared at me with dark brooding eyes. His wife looked equally stern. Her black hair was parted in the middle and severely pulled back. The only one with any appearance of softness was the daughter, Hannah. Her round face and dimpled chin promised better looks than either parent.

'I wonder why they were buried here,' I said. Crystal looked at me with her big blue eyes and I felt a pleasant sensation wash over me. She came up close and put her hands on my chest

'Nice,' she said. I put my hand on her breast. 'Nice,' I said. We were enjoying replaying yesterday's game but this time, Rick wasn't around to interrupt. I slid my hand under her sheer top and found her bikini bra. I fondled her breast. She closed her eyes and sighed. Then we were kissing. I looked at the ground beneath us. It was rough and stony. I picked her up, carried her to the nearby grave, and gently laid her on the soft grass.

The body I had been coveting was now mine. Crystal's passion was as strong as mine and she seemed hungry for me. Our love-making was intensely emotional. We climaxed together and the euphoria went on for ages after. We lay side by side without speaking for several minutes. I was more convinced than ever that I had found my 'forever' girl. I took her hand in mind, brought it to my lips and kissed it.

'No ring?' I asked looking at the smooth tapered fingers.

'Rick and I aren't married.'

'Why are you with him?'

'He's good to me.'

'He doesn't seem very attentive.'

'That's his way when we're with company. Alone, he can't do enough for me.'

'Do you love him?'

'No, but he made me feel secure.'

'Why would a beautiful girl like you be insecure?'

'It goes back a long way...to the beginning, actually. I was an abandoned baby. My mother walked into a Sydney maternity hospital and put me in an empty cot. It wasn't long before the staff realised I was an intruder. Apparently, I was on the news and in the papers. No one claimed me. After a few months, I was put up for adoption.'

'Your mother must have loved you. She made sure she left you somewhere safe. Not like some babies that get dumped on doorsteps or thrown in garbage bins.'

I glanced sideways at Crystal. Her expression was soft and she gazed up at the clouds.

'Yes, she loved me.' A small smile crept onto her face. 'Anyway, I'm no longer insecure.'

'Then you won't need Rick any longer.'

'You're probably right.'

'What are your adoptive parents like?'

'I never ever felt part of them. I don't think they loved me. They were both over fifty when they got me.'

I whistled. 'They must have pulled some strings to get you. From what I know, there are age limits for adopting parents. Fifty seems pretty old.'

'Well, they're both dead now. Mother had a brain tumour last year and Dad died a few months later.'

'I'm sorry.'

'Don't be sorry. I'm not.' There was a short pause and Crystal spoke again. 'Have you been unfaithful to Shelly before?'

'No,' I said truthfully.

'Will you regret it?'

'No, will you?'

'How long have you been with Shelly?' she asked, avoiding my question.

'About a year.'

'How did you meet?'

'In a club. I was with Ben. Shelly was alone. I made a play. The rest is history.'

'So, what was *her* history?'

'Parents dead, no relatives. She lived in a unit at the Cross.'

'Is that all you know about her?'

'What else is there to know?'

'I think you should have learned more.'

I turned my head and looked into her eyes. 'Why?'

'Forget it,' she said.

I kissed her cheek. 'I don't want this to be a one-time stand, Crystal. I want to see you when we get back.'

'What about Shelly?'

'I just realised I don't love Shelly. If I did, I wouldn't feel this way about you.'

'I would like to see you too, Brett. But let's keep this a secret for the time being. I don't want to cause any trouble on the boat.'

'Okay.' I closed my eyes. The sun remained beneath my lids creating splashes of pink, purple and gold.

After a while, Crystal sat up, and slowly took in her surroundings. 'Oh God, we're on a grave! We did it on a grave!'

'It was nice and soft.' I grinned, thinking she was joking.

'We have desecrated her grave,' she sobbed. I could see she was serious.

'Crystal, there's no one there.' I sat up.

'Don't you believe the spirit goes on after death?'

'I don't think I do. But if the spirit does go on, you can be sure it's not down there. I turned my head and quickly checked the name on the headstone. 'Why, Hannah Edwards is probably way up there sitting on a nice sunny cloud playing the harp right now.'

'It just doesn't seem right.' She sighed as she put her head on my shoulder. In that instant, I thought I saw a flash of red behind the bushes near the end of the track. I decided it was probably a parrot.

'I guess we should start thinking about getting back. We don't want them sending out a search party. It's best we go separately,' Crystal said.

'You go back down the track and I'll walk around the island. I'll get back to the beach at the other end,' I said.

'It'll take you forever to walk around the island,' she said softly.

'I've just received an enormous spurt of energy. I could climb Everest right now.'

'Well, don't get lost.'

The walk took nearly two hours and it was late afternoon before I finally returned to the beach. There was no sign of Ben, Steve, Jaz, or Danni. Rick was sitting reading a book and Shelly and Crystal were standing near the shoreline deep in conversation. It bothered me to see this and I wondered what they were talking about. I then noticed the dinghy heading back to the beach with Steve at the helm. I wandered down to the dinghy as it came ashore.

'Where are the others?' I asked as we pulled the dinghy onto the sand.

'They're on board.' Steve waved to Shelly. She strutted over, gave me a killing look, and climbed wordlessly into the dinghy. Rick and Crystal wandered over and climbed in after her.

Everyone seemed a bit subdued on this our last night. I think the three days of heavy drinking had taken their toll.

I had trouble keeping my eyes away from Crystal. She was avoiding my glances.

Shelly was grim and in a foul temper. She ignored me and I was grateful.

People were helping themselves to snacks and as usual, there was a line to the shower. I found some biscuits and cheese and poured myself a beer.

'I've bought an Ouija board,' said Danni. Let's see what spirits we can invoke.'

'I think we've already invoked more spirits than we can handle,' said Jaz looking sidewise at Steve's bourbon drink.

'C'mon, it'll be good fun,' said Danni who already looked 'four sheets to the wind.'

Danni set up the board and placed a wineglass upside down in the middle. Jaz sat at the table and pulled Steve down beside her.

'Why don't you all grow up?' sneered Rick.

Although I had no intention of joining the 'Ouija', I plonked myself down the minute Rick made his comment. Ben, too, looked irritated by Rick and sat next to Danni. Both Crystal and Shelly seemed to have reservations and stood back. Crystal watched Rick as he stomped off. She then slid in beside me.

'C'mon Shelly,' called Danni. Shelly reluctantly sat on the other side of the table next to Steve.

'Lower the lights,' demanded Danni.

'They can't get any lower,' said Jaz.

Danni held out her hands. 'We must all hold hands.' she said.

Silently, we grabbed at each other.

'Is anyone there?' called Danni. 'For yes, knock once. '

We all sat waiting.  Steve started giggling, Ben let out a snort and I had trouble containing myself. Danni and Jaz sat with upturned faces and closed eyes.  I turned to Crystal with a grin.  Her eyes were wide open and I noticed a furrow on her brow. She didn't return my gaze.

Then there was a knock that seemed to come from under the table.

'The spirits have answered us.  We can now put our fingers on the glass,' said Danni.  'Who is with us?' she asked.

We all had a finger on the upturned glass.  It was still for nearly thirty seconds then it started moving slowly in tight circles.  The circles widened and the glass moved faster.  It started sweeping across the board from one side to another.  I knew I wasn't guiding it, but as for the others, I wasn't sure.  It kept sweeping across the table and finally landed on the letter 'H'. There was a pause and it took off again.  It landed on the letter 'A' and then swooped onto the letter 'N'.

'I don't like this.  We should leave them alone,' said Crystal, standing.

'You can't break the circle, Crystal,' said Danni.

'I *have* broken it.'  Crystal sat on one of the side lounges and picked up a magazine.

We all continued with our fingers on the glass.  It was still for a few seconds and then I saw Steve give it a push.  I knew he was playing 'silly-buggers'. Danni saw it too.

'You're cheating, Steve.'

'I think the spirit has packed his bag and gone

home,' said Steve.

'Well, if that's the case, I'm off for a shower.'

I got up, grabbed a fresh set of shorts from my plastic bag, and made for the shower room. The water was warm. I enjoyed the sensation of it washing over my salty body but I felt a bit sad that I was also washing away some of Crystal.

When I joined the others, there was a lot of fussing going on. Jaz was mopping coffee off the table. 'Trust our rotten luck to score the table tonight, just when it gets covered in coffee,' she grizzled.

I joined the group. 'Your coffee is on the bench,' said Shelly in a tight voice. The coffee was lukewarm but I drank it in two gulps.

Everyone started making sleeping arrangements. We had the side lounges tonight. Shelly had already set hers up and was taking off her shoes.

I couldn't see Crystal and guessed she could be on the deck. I wandered out and heard her voice. She was nursing her cup and leaning on the railing. I came up beside her and felt a tingling in my shoulder as it touched hers.

'Talking to yourself?' I grinned.

'Oh no, I was talking to Hannah. She was here. You scared her away.'

'Hannah? What are you saying, Crystal?' My grin quickly disappeared and instead, I felt gravely unsettled. Crystal's eyes were misty and she spoke softly.

'Hannah Edwards came to me through the Ouija. I told her I was so sorry we had desecrated her grave. She said it was okay and she'd see me very soon.'

'Crystal, you didn't see Hannah. I think you should get some sleep. We'll talk about all this in the morning.' I put my arm around her shoulder. I didn't have a clue what else to do. Crystal said nothing but tipped her coffee into the river and walked inside.

In the cabin, there was noisy activity. Steve had converted the table to a double bed and Jaz was washing up cups and glasses. It was only eleven but I was ready for sleep.

It wasn't long before we were all settled and the curtains were drawn. I gazed into the blackness and thought about Crystal. Her strange words on the deck concerned me greatly. But I decided to deal with this in the morning. Instead, I thought about our time together on the island and remembered the softness of her body and the taste and fragrance of her skin. I became aroused just thinking about it. Tonight, she and Rick were in a cabin again. I felt a stab of jealousy, and wished I was there with her behind that curtain. Although my bunk was grossly uncomfortable, I fell asleep after a short while.

I awoke to see a face above mine. It was evil and malicious. It was Hannah Edwards. She had a pillow and slammed it down on my face. I tried to push it off but her strength was incredible. I was suffocating. At last, when I felt I would die, I managed to push the pillow away. My throat was dry and there was a pounding in my chest. I felt sweat running down my neck. It took a while for me to realise I had been dreaming.

The cabin was in total darkness and I could hear the steady sounds of snoring. Then I heard a

knocking noise on the side of the boat and thought I
heard a soft female voice. The dinghy was at the stern
so I reasoned it couldn't be that causing the knocking. I
wanted desperately to check the deck and tried to get my
legs to work. But they felt like lead and wouldn't move. I
pulled aside the porthole curtain and there it was again—
the big cruiser. I fell back into a deep sleep.

The next morning, I was awakened by loud
voices. Rick was shouting. I tumbled out of bed and
almost met him head-on. He was tearing around like a
madman.

'What's up?' I asked.

Rick didn't reply.

Danni was pulling the rollers out of her hair. 'It's
Crystal, she's disappeared,' she screamed.

Instinctively I went to the cabin and pulled aside
the curtain. It didn't take long to know that Crystal was
not on board.

'Could she have swum across to the island?'
asked Danni.

'She can't fucking swim,' yelled Rick.

I felt sick inside as I remembered the noise I'd
heard during the night. Had Crystal fallen overboard? I
was seized with panic and, without thinking, dived off the
side. I swam around the keel but the visibility was poor.
I tried diving further down to the river bed, but the water
was too deep and I needed to surface for more air. Rick
was also in the water but he was just floundering and
splashing around. He clambered back on board after a
short while.

I dived again and again. And then I heard Danni

shouting that the dinghy had gone.  In my panic, I hadn't noticed it missing.  This brought me hope and I told myself that Crystal was okay.  She had taken off in the dinghy and was probably floating down the river.  I climbed back on board.  Shelly and Rick were standing together on the deck. As I passed, Rick grabbed me by the shoulder. 'You're responsible for this, you fuckwit.' I felt his spittle hit my face.  I wiped it off slowly.

'What are you on about?' I shook off his grip.

'Don't play the innocent with me. I know what you did on the island. It's all in her diary. You fucked her on a grave.'

'Go to hell, you moron.'  I pushed past him and climbed the stairs to the flight deck and joined Steve and Jaz.

'I've called Marine Rescue, they should be here soon,' said Steve.

'Crystal's probably lost control of the dinghy.  I think we should start searching for her,' said Jaz.

'Marine Rescue told us to stay put.  They've got our bearings,' said Steve.

We sat quietly waiting.  All the time I was thinking about what Rick had said.  Somehow, he knew what had happened between me and Crystal.  But I couldn't imagine Crystal writing about it in her diary.

A marine rescue helicopter arrived and hovered overhead making an ear-splitting racket.  It swept away and then a marine rescue boat came into view.  Within a few minutes, it pulled alongside and two men boarded. We were given the news none of us wanted to hear.  The dinghy was found downstream—empty.  We were briefly questioned and the boat was searched.

Another launch approached, dropping divers into the river and towing the empty dinghy behind. We were told to return to the marina.

On the journey back, we were all quiet and burdened with our own thoughts. I saw Danni crying into her handkerchief. Rick sat like a stone, chain-smoking.

Jaz suddenly spoke. 'Why did you throw Crystal's diary overboard, Rick?'

Rick remained silent and his jaw tightened.

'I saw you. Why?' Jaz persisted.

Rick got up and lumbered out to the deck.

At the base, we were met by three detectives. Two boarded the cruiser and requested that we leave our things on board. The third man led us to a small room attached to the marina. We were questioned separately and our statements recorded.

Detective Collins was a middle-aged guy with a sour face and zero personality. 'Did you hear anything during the night?' he asked.

'I heard a knocking noise on the starboard side. I also think I heard a voice.'

'Did you investigate?'

'No.'

'Why not?'

'I felt very tired. My legs wouldn't work. I had just woken from a bad dream.'

The guy threw me a scornful look. I guess I must have sounded like a weak wimp.

'Was the voice male or female?'

My mind went back to that moment. I recalled the

sheer terror the dream had created and my feelings of helplessness both asleep and awake. 'I think it was female,' I whispered.

'What?'

'I think it was female,' I repeated in a loud voice. *Were there any arguments? Was anyone taking drugs?* I answered all his questions. He folded up his notebook and focused on me with narrowed eyes. 'Anything else you can tell me?'

'I saw a big cruiser on all three nights. Each night it was berthed some distance away. I can't be sure, but I think it was the same cruiser every time.' Collins cast me an inscrutable look, opened his book and wrote.

After an hour or so we were allowed to leave. All our stuff had been moved off the boat and was lying on the jetty for collection. I had no doubt that it had been searched.

I located our bags and looked around for Shelly. She was talking to Rick. They walked over together.

'You bastard,' Rick spat, raising his fist. I blocked the punch and pushed him. He stumbled back. I was stronger and younger and knew I could flatten him.

'You're responsible. She's dead and you're responsible,' he yelled.

I pointed my finger at him. 'You watch it man, just watch it.' I turned to Shelly. 'Coming, Shelly?' Shelly wordlessly followed me to the car.

We drove in silence all the way home.

I tried to get my thoughts into some sort of order. Crystal was missing. Where was she? I had made love to her less than twenty-four hours earlier. I felt an acute feeling of pain and sadness and loss. My head was spinning and my thinking was jumbled and scattered.

When we pulled into our garage, I looked at Shelly. 'That Rick's a prick.'

'Everything he said was true. I despise you,' she hissed. She sprang out of the car and headed for the lift. I took the stairs. Inside the apartment, I heard noises coming from the bedroom. I tried the door but it was locked. Five minutes later Shelly came out dragging a suitcase. Her eyes were blazing and she spoke through clenched teeth. 'I'm leaving you. I never want to see you again.' She left the apartment, slamming the door behind her.

I sank into the lounge and pulled a cushion over my face.

*

The days passed and there was no call from Shelly. I had no idea where she had gone. I really didn't care as my thoughts were now only of Crystal. My emotions were suffocating me and there was a sharp pain in my gut that wouldn't go away.

Then Danni phoned. 'Shelly told us what happened between you and Crystal! I think Crystal killed herself and I think you're partly to blame.'

'Think what you like.' I slammed down the phone.

Then Jaz called. 'I want to contact Shelly,' she said flatly.

'She's gone.'

'Where?'

'I don't know.'

'Shelly told me what happened on the island between you and Crystal. I think Crystal's suicide is tied in with it. She had significant emotional problems and I don't think she could handle that sort of thing.' Jaz hung up without a goodbye.

I thought it weird that neither Steve nor Ben called. It was their wives who had done the dirty work. Shelly's vendetta was creating a rift between me and my friends. I felt hurt and puzzled by their reaction. Crystal's disappearance had a traumatic effect on everyone. It was clear they all believed she had committed suicide. But why were they blaming me? Maybe they each had their own little pocket of guilt.

Possibly Jaz felt guilty because she had tried so hard to get the eight-berth cruiser. If she hadn't, none of this would have happened. And Danni, she was the one who invited Crystal to come. How must she feel? And Ben, what if he hadn't gone to that particular island? What if he had taken the boat somewhere else? Would that have made a difference?

I called Steve and Ben. Neither was over-friendly. Neither suggested we meet for a drink or chat. I mulled over this and felt wounded. The whole ghastly thing started haunting me. Maybe Crystal *had* killed herself. Maybe I *was* responsible. And then I started feeling guilty.

*

It was now getting dark. I had sat on my deck for two hours after Danni's call. I had finally allowed myself to recall the entire set of events from the time I'd met Crystal right up to her disappearance. If I went to

crystal

the memorial service, what would I do and say?

Tonight, since Danni's call, I had faced my demons. I left my deck, and realised there and then, that I might have to go to Sydney and face them again.

*

# CHAPTER 3
## *Stephanie 2015*

Stephanie Darrieux stood waiting. A passing car caused her to pull back into the shadows. The tall, damp grass on the verge brushed her calves. This increased the chill that had slowly invaded her body since leaving the comforting warmth of the Poplars Arms. The bus stop, faintly illuminated by an overhead street light, was in front of the Uniting Church. Stephanie knew a girl seen alone in this neighbourhood, could be inviting trouble. The shadows were her refuge.

It was late May and the coldness cloaked her shoulders. She wished she had accepted the cardigan her mother had tried to force on her earlier that night. But where was Jordan? She felt angry and irritated. It was bad enough that he tagged along with her every Friday night. But to go running off like that when the bus was due!

She loved these Friday gatherings, the live music and the dancing. As a group, the university guys could be funny and entertaining. On dates, they seemed different—intense, awkward.

She enjoyed the camaraderie and particularly liked Magda Kasmarik who had recently become her best friend. Magda had a great sense of humour and could put Stephanie into fits of laughter with her atrocious impersonations of the various lecturers and students in the Law School.

While Stephanie socialised with her Uni friends, Jordan met his schoolmates. At first, she protested to her parents. Having a kid brother tag along was humiliating, but her father thought it was a good idea. Henri Darrieux hung to the old belief that young women should not go out alone at night. He was the eldest son of French parents whose strict mores had been visited on all their six children. Henri's youngest sister Louisa had not been allowed out until she was twenty-one years old. Then, in total fear of an unknown world, she turned her back on it and became a Carmelite nun. Henri Darrieux had adopted some of his parents' beliefs and had placed them on his own two children.

Even now at twenty-two years of age, Stephanie still didn't quite feel like an adult. She had gone straight from high school to university and it seemed that her life was just one long procession of classrooms and study. She had dated various guys since leaving school. Her pretty face had attracted endless invitations. But she had never accepted a second offer from the same person. The truth was that none of these young men attracted or interested her. She had to admit that having Jordan along on Fridays wasn't all that bad. While he was there, she didn't have to fight off offers to 'see her home.'

At the pub, Jordan would group off with his mates and didn't bother Stephanie during the night.

The band played until after one but she and

Jordan always caught the 12.10 bus which got them home twenty minutes later.

Tonight, was the same as any other Friday. The music had been great and although Stephanie was having a ball, she rounded Jordan up before midnight.

They had just crossed the road from the pub when Stephanie heard a short whistle. She and Jordan turned together. Stephanie saw a shadowy figure on the other side of the road, near the entrance to a narrow laneway.

'I'll meet you at the bus stop.' Jordan said running back across the road in the direction of the lane. Stephanie was angry but continued walking.

More than five minutes passed. Now she was starting to worry. What if the bus should come and he still wasn't here? Would she catch it? She knew she couldn't leave him. It would be hours before another bus came. She had her mobile in her bag but that didn't help as Jordan didn't carry one.

'Come on Jordan', she whispered as she hugged her arms into her body trying to ward off the chilling air. She looked into the churchyard. The big building was silhouetted against the night sky and the headstones on the graves rose upwards like ghostly sentinels. A figure appeared from around the bend. As it passed under a street light, she saw that it was a man. He was half running, half walking seeming to be loping as if crippled. She was disappointed that it wasn't Jordan. *Where in hell's name is he?*

As the figure approached, she drew further back into the shadows, suddenly feeling afraid. Then when the figure came under the nearby streetlight, she saw the white stricken face. It *was* Jordan. Why was he running so funny? Stephanie stepped out of her shadowy sanctuary and Jordan collapsed against her. He was breathing heavily. 'Jordan, what's the matter?' He started sliding slowly to the ground. It was then, under the streetlight, that Stephanie saw the blood. His shirt was soaked and gleaming red. Her hands suddenly felt wet and sticky. They were covered in blood.

Stephanie screamed for help and fell down beside him. 'Jordie, what happened?' She saw his eyes widen like those of a frightened animal.

'Stabbed,' he muttered. Stephanie frantically pulled out her mobile and hit 000. Her voice was high pitched and the words tumbled out. 'My brother's been stabbed! He's badly hurt. Please send an ambulance!'

'Where are you?'

'Outside the Uniting Church in Gordon Street, Annandale.'

'What's your name?'

'Stephanie Darrieux.'

'How do you spell that?'

'For Christ's sake, what does it matter how I spell my name? Get someone here!' Stephanie looked down at her brother. A small cough sent a gush of blood from his mouth. Stephanie groaned. 'I think he's dying.'

'Okay, love, just hang in there. Someone will be there soon.'

'Who did it, Jordie?' Stephanie asked. Jordan's lips were moving but nothing was coming out. His foot gave a little kick. Then he was still. His eyes were wide open, staring straight at her, but seeing nothing.

The ambulance arrived within minutes. One of the officers knelt beside Stephanie and began checking Jordan's pulse. Stephanie was oblivious to her surroundings. She cradled Jordan's head in her lap and prayed to God to save him. The bus drew into the kerb, and inquisitive passengers peered out. A few people had gathered and stood by watching. Stephanie remained kneeling on the cold, hard footpath. Three police cars arrived in quick succession and Jordan was put on a stretcher. Within seconds the ambulance pulled away with its siren blaring. Two policemen helped Stephanie to her feet.

'Do you know that boy?' asked the older man.

'He's my brother.'

'His name?'

'Jordan Darrieux.'

'And you are?'

'Stephanie Darrieux.'

'Did you see who attacked him?'

'No. He went back.'

'Back where?'

'To the hotel.'

'The Poplars?'

'Yes.

'He was attacked there?'

'I don't know where he was attacked. He came running up the street. He was bleeding.' Stephanie started feeling giddy. The younger policeman caught her as her knees started buckling.

'Take her to the car,' said the older man.

Stephanie heard a voice shouting, 'Trace that blood

trail and talk to all these people. You two go to the Poplars Arms and talk to the people there.'

At the police station, Stephanie was given a hot drink. Inspector Manning sat opposite her. The young policeman stood nearby.

'Can you tell me anything that might help us find your brother's attacker?'

'How is my brother?'

'I'm very sorry—he died.'

Stephanie's heart lurched. She felt numb and cold.

'Where are your parents?'

'At home, waiting,' she whispered.

'Do you want to phone them?' He pushed the phone towards her. Stephanie called the familiar number. Her mother answered. Stephanie had prayed that her father would answer. She felt like stone as she spoke.

'Mama.'

'Where are you? Your father and I are worried half to death.'

'Mama, it's Jordan—he's dead!' Stephanie heard her mother's anguished cry. That cry would ring in her ears for months to come.

*

The autopsy revealed that Jordan had died from multiple wounds to his chest and throat. It also revealed that he had amphetamines in his system. The weeks that followed were shattering. There were questions and more questions. *What did Stephanie see that night? Did Stephanie know that*

*Jordan took drugs?'* *Did she know where Jordan got his drugs?*

One of the policemen who seemed always to be part of this questioning was the young man who had attended the scene that night. Stephanie learned his name was Brendan Lloyd. He seemed caring and concerned and Stephanie warmed to his compassion.

In all her interviews, Stephanie gave the same answers. She saw nothing other than the shadowy figure near the laneway and she didn't know where Jordan got the amphetamines.

The police questioned both Jordan's and Stephanie's pub groups. Nothing came out of the questioning except that three people left the hotel around the same time as Stephanie and Jordan. The police had questioned these three and were satisfied that they were not involved.

After a month, there was still no lead. Jordan had been buried, and the notes of condolences had finally stopped. Henri and Estelle were quietly grieving. Estelle's lovely auburn hair had suddenly become streaked with grey.

Stephanie eventually returned to university. Her hard work earlier in the year stood her in good stead and she was able to quickly pick up the lost work. Magda had been supportive throughout and would often suggest a coffee after lectures. Here, she listened quietly while Stephanie would talk and cry.

Six weeks passed and Stephanie and Magda were sipping their coffees in the university canteen. 'I'm going to the pub this Friday. Want to come?' asked

Magda, looking into her coffee.  When Stephanie didn't answer, Magda turned to face her.  Their eyes met.  'Well?' she asked.

'Have you been there...since?'

'No.  But I think we should go.  We enjoyed it once.  We'll enjoy it again!'

'I can't go back there.'

'Give it a try.  You can always clear out if it gets too much.'

*

It was now mid-winter.  Stephanie searched for Magda as she entered from the outside cold into the warmth and noise of the hotel.  Magda's hand shot up when she spotted Stephanie.  The group greeted her warmly.  Someone put a glass of vodka and orange in front of her.  Her friends were careful not to mention Jordan.  During the night, Stephanie found herself laughing.  It was the first time she had laughed since that dreadful night.  Magda caught her eye and they exchanged smiles.  Stephanie accepted a lift home from one of the guys.  She was grateful he didn't try to kiss her.

Although the home was like a mausoleum, Stephanie started feeling a part of the human race again.  The pain was still there but she could now at least think.  She thought a lot about Jordan and how he died.  But most of all, she thought about his killer.  She called Constable Lloyd.  'What's happening with the investigation?' she asked.

'Nothing.  I'm sorry but it seems that no one saw anything that night.'

'The three people who left the hotel around the same time as us, who were they?'

'Two of them were in Jordan's group. The other one was just a customer.'

'Can you give me their names?'

'Are you at home now? I'll be off duty at three. I can call in.'

'Yes. But my parents have had enough of police. I'll meet you somewhere.'

'Okay, where?'

'The coffee shop up the road, the Green Inn.'

'I know it. Three-thirty?'

'See you there.' Stephanie pulled off her track-suit and put on her good cream slacks. She added an emerald-green jumper. She knew it suited her. It matched her eyes perfectly. She also knew she was attracted to Constable Lloyd. She liked the strength and broadness of his face and the warmth in his brown eyes.

Brendan Lloyd was seated in a booth at the coffee shop when Stephanie arrived. She slid in beside him. The waitress came and they ordered flat whites. Brendan looked at her for a long while before speaking. 'Do you mind if I call you Stephanie?'

'Not at all. I would like it. And you are Brendan?'

'Yes.' He shifted in his seat for a second or two and then placed a flat briefcase on the table. He took out a laptop, brought it to life, and tapped in some details.

'Joseph Blakely and Edmond Khoury,' he said squinting at the screen. 'They were in Jordan's group that night and they left the hotel around the same time as you. Do you know them?'

'I have heard of Joe Blakely but I don't remember ever meeting him. I don't think he was a particular friend of Jordan's. But I know Eddie Khoury. He's been to our house. He and Jordan are...were, in the same class at school. Eddie lives in the next street. He came a few times to the house and they played on their computers.'

'What did they play?'

'All those silly games, Dungeons and Dragons, that sort of thing. Who was the third person?'

'Tony Mifsud. He was alone that night. The barman noticed him leaving when you and Jordan left. His car was parked opposite the hotel and the barman saw him drive off. It appears he left the area before Jordan was attacked. There's nothing to link him with Jordan's death.'

'What about the other two? Where did they go?"

'Joe Blakely stayed the night at the Khoury house. The father vouches for the boys—said they arrived home soon after twelve and they all sat around watching television until after one.'

Their flat whites came and they sipped silently. 'What's happening now?' asked Stephanie.

'We've hit a blank wall.'

'There must be something you can do to find the killer.'

'Did you know Jordan was on drugs?'

'I've answered that question before. I knew he had the odd smoke, but nothing else. He said he got the dope from a mate. I don't know anything about amphetamines.'

'Do you know which mate sold him the stuff?'

'No.   I've answered that question before too,'
Stephanie said sharply.   She immediately regretted her
harsh tone and spoke again in a soft voice. 'Most of the
kids were into grass.  Jordan never seemed spaced out.
He seemed to handle it okay.'  There was a short silence.
'Have you found the weapon?'

'No.'

Stephanie felt dejected.  It seemed to her that the
police were now treating Jordan's murder as an
unsolved crime.  She decided there and then that she
would start making her own enquiries.

'I know where Eddie Khoury lives but could you
give me the addresses of the other two?'

'Why?'

'I'd like to talk with them.'

'You could annoy them.  They have already talked
to us.'

'If they're innocent, as you say they are, they
shouldn't mind.  They should be happy to help.'

Brendan slipped the laptop away and looked at
Stephanie questioningly. 'What do you do at university?'

'I'm studying law.'

'Apart from Friday nights, do you ever take time
out?'

'For what?'

'To have dinner with a policeman.'

'Is that an invitation?'

'It is.  Can I take you to dinner this Saturday?'

'Yes, that would be nice.  But will you give me
those addresses?'

'I'll give them to you on Saturday night.'

Brendon Lloyd had been attracted to this beautiful girl from the first moment. He admired her courage and felt dejected that he couldn't supply any answers to her tragedy. It was a long time since he had felt such an attraction and he was determined to make an all-out effort to impress.

On the following Saturday, Brendon checked himself in his full-length mirror. He noted with satisfaction that the creases in his grey slacks had been pressed to a knife edge, his smart new navy jacket contrasted well with his crisp white shirt and his shoes had been polished to a gleaming finish. All this gave him a measure of confidence.

Stephanie introduced Brendan to her parents, even though he had met them in the course of the investigation. Henri shook his hand but said nothing. Estelle stood silently in the background. Her grieving was such that at times Stephanie thought her mother might be losing her mind.

Stephanie hurried Brendan out of the house. He drove to a very up-market restaurant in a neighbouring suburb. When booking, he had requested a corner table which he knew was quiet and private.

Brendon steered her to the table.

'This is lovely.' Stephanie's eyes were bright with excitement.

'Wait till you taste the food.' The wine waiter came with the menu. Brendon perused it.

'White or red?' he asked with raised eyebrows.

'Either. You choose.'

Brendan ordered the wine and then sat back

appraising her. Tonight, she looked especially lovely. Again, she was wearing green and he noticed how it matched her eyes. 'You have beautiful eyes,' he said.

She smiled as she put her hand on his. 'Are you going to give me those addresses?'
Brendan searched in his pocket and withdrew a piece of paper. He handed it to her. 'Thank you.' she smiled.

'What will you say to them?'

'I'm not sure.'

'None of them have records. There's no reason for us to think they were involved.' He took a sip of his wine and tried to loosen the tension he was feeling. Discussing the case was suddenly causing him undue anxiety. 'Let's talk about happier things.'

'Okay. What made you become a policeman?'

'My father was a policeman, as was my grandfather. I never thought of anything else.'

The night passed pleasantly and Stephanie drank more wine than usual. She was steadily warming towards Brendan. He was the nicest guy she had ever dated.

They left the restaurant around eleven. When they arrived back at Stephanie's house Brendan parked his car a little down the road away from the glare of the street light. Stephanie wondered what he would do next. For the first time ever, she wanted to be kissed. Surprisingly, Brendan lit a cigarette. He hadn't smoked the entire night and this came as a surprise to her.

'I didn't know you smoked,' she said.

'Only when I'm nervous.'

'Why are you nervous?'

'I want to kiss you and I'm not sure if I should.'

'I think you should.'

Brendan stubbed out the cigarette and took her in his arms. The sharp tang of his aftershave and the slightly smoky scent on his breath increased Stephanie's desire. He kissed her gently. She compared his kiss to the rough kisses of the university boys who tried to poke their tongues in her mouth and grab at her breasts. Brendan did none of this. His kisses were sweet and gentle.

Stephanie went to sleep that night glowing with excitement. Was Brendan 'Mr Right?'

The next day was Sunday. Stephanie told Henri that she was going to Mass and asked if she could borrow the car. Even though Henri and Estelle had not attended Mass for several years, they were disappointed when both Stephanie and Jordan stopped going a year or so ago. Henri was only too willing to lend his car. Maybe his daughter was resuming her religious duties.

Stephanie went to the nine o'clock Mass. The church was packed. She couldn't help noticing the numerous white and grey heads in the congregation. *Not too many young people*, she thought. This realisation comforted her. Maybe her reluctance to attend church wasn't so unusual after all. She left soon after the Communion and headed out to Joey Blakeley's place.

The house was semi-detached with a tiny front yard. A cracked concrete path led to the front door.

Stephanie knocked and waited. Close by, two Indian minor birds pecked the ground, brazenly ignoring her proximity.   The door opened halfway.  A thin, worn-looking woman glared suspiciously at her.

'My name is Stephanie Darrieux.  Could I speak with Joe, please?'

'He's in bed.  What do you want?'

'It's about my brother Jordan.'

The woman's face tightened and she pressed her lips together.  'He's told the cops everything he knows.'

'I thought perhaps if I talked to Joe, he might remember something.'

'I'll see if he's awake.'  The woman left leaving Stephanie standing at the door.  She returned a minute later.  'He's getting up.  Come in.'

Stephanie followed her down a narrow hallway to a room containing a shabby lounge suite, a television set and two small coffee tables.

'Sit down,' said Frances Blakely.

Stephanie sat uncomfortably on one of the single chairs.

Five minutes later Joe Blakely entered, scratching his untidy ginger head.   He glared at Stephanie through tired, bloodshot eyes.

'Hi, Joe.  I'm Stephanie, Jordan's sister.'

'I know who you are.  What do you want?'

'I just want you to tell me all that happened that night, at the pub.'

'I've told the cops everything,' he said, collapsing into a worn lounge chair.

'Yeah, and they even made him go down to the station. They had no right to do that. Joey's done nothin' wrong,' said Frances.

'Piss off, Mum. Make a cup of tea or somethin'.'

Frances threw a scornful look at Joey and left the room. Stephanie was glad. Having his mother around might interfere with Joey's memory processes.

'What time did you get to the pub?'

'Around eight-thirty. Jordan was already there.'

'Who else was there?'

'Not the usual crowd. There was a big party in Leichhardt and lots of the guys had been invited. There were only eight of us there that night.'

'Were they all still there when you and Eddie left?'

'No, two blokes left at ten. They were going to crash the party.'

'So, when you left at twelve, there were only three people from your group still there?'

'Yeah.'

'You were still there when I came over for Jordan, and I remember seeing Eddie Khoury.'

'Yeah, but we followed you out the door. The night was a flop. None of the girls showed. They were all at the party.'

'Where did you go, after you left the pub?'

'Eddie had his dad's jalopy and he'd parked it around in Graham Street.'

'So, you had to pass the laneway?'

'Yes. But neither of us saw anyone there. When we got to the car, we drove it around the block and back up to the main road. We didn't pass the lane again.'

'Did you see another man leaving the pub at the same time?'

'No.'

'When you were walking to the car, did you hear a whistle?'

Joe Blakely wiped a pale, freckled hand across his mouth. 'Don't think so. It's a noisy street, lots of traffic.'

'There wasn't much traffic at that time.'

'I don't remember hearing a whistle. I was half-pissed by then anyway.'

'During the night, was there anyone, outside your group, that Jordan spoke to?'

'No. But there was a dude sitting near us. He was pretending to read the paper, but we reckoned he was listening in on us.'

'Why do you say he was pretending to read the paper?'

'He never turned the page once. I was watching him.'

'What did he look like?'

'Short, thin, Leb-looking, older than us.'

'Did you mention him to the police?'

'I think I might have.'

'What time did you get to the Khoury house?'

'About quarter past twelve. Eddie's old man was watching the footy replay. We sat and watched it with him. We all turned in around one-thirty.'

Stephanie stood. 'Thanks, Joey.'

'I'm sorry I didn't go to the funeral. I wanted to, but—.'

'That's okay.' Stephanie stood. 'I'll see myself out.' She left the house with mixed feelings.

Nothing much had come from her talk with Joe, except the reference to the man with the newspaper.

She then headed to the Khoury house. A short, stocky woman with dark eyes set beneath heavy eyelids opened the door. 'Yes?'

'I'm Stephanie Darrieux, Jordan's sister. Could I speak with Eddie please?'

'Why you want talk with Edmond?' Her accent was heavy.

'I want to talk to him about Jordan.'

Without a word, she turned inside. Stephanie stood in the open doorway. After a few seconds, the woman reappeared.

'Come,' she said with an incline of her head.

The Khoury house was a small free-standing federation cottage. It reeked of Middle Eastern cooking odours. Stephanie followed the woman to a room halfway down the hallway. 'Sit,' the woman muttered as she turned and left the room. Stephanie sat uncomfortably on a chair that was sagging and soiled. She looked around the small room. The sparse furniture was old and shabby. A worn rug partly covered the timber flooring. A large black cat lay asleep on the coffee table.

Eddie Khoury stood in the doorway. He, like Joey, was dishevelled and sleepy-looking.

'Hi, Eddie. I hope I didn't get you up.'

'You did.'

'Sorry. I wanted to talk about the night Jordan was killed.'

'I've told the cops everything I know.' Eddie

flopped onto the lounge opposite her. He flung one leg over the chair's arm and stared insolently at her through hooded dark eyes.

'Yes, but sometimes things come back, things you might have forgotten. Joe Blakely mentioned a man sitting near your group in the pub. Joe said he was pretending to read a newspaper. Did you notice him?'

'Yeah.'

'Do you think he was spying on you?'

'Yeah, I do.'

'Did he talk to anyone?'

'Only Jordan.'

This news stunned Stephanie. 'He talked to Jordan? When?'

'Well, I *think* he talked to Jordan. He followed Jordan to the dunny. I went in later and he and Jordan were standing at the basins. It looked like they'd been talking. But they didn't talk while I was there. Jordan walked out and the guy followed.'

'Did you tell this to the police?'

'Yeah, I told the head guy.'

'When you went back to the group, what was happening?'

'Nothin'. Jordan was yakkin' to Bugsy.'

'And the man?'

'He was up at the bar gettin' a beer.'

'Did he talk to Jordan again?'

Eddie shook his head.

'Did you ask Jordan about the man?'

'Yeah, I did. Jordan said he'd never seen him before. I found out later the guy's name is Mifsud.'

'Mifsud! He was the other person who left when we did. Did you see where he went? Can you tell me anything at all that might help me find Jordie's killer?'

Eddie sullenly shook his head.

'I knew Jordan smoked pot and now the police tell us he was doing amphetamines too. Do you know anything about that?' Eddie looked at her with his liquid black eyes. For a moment Stephanie thought he was going to speak. Then he hung his head and shook it slowly.

Stephanie stood. 'Thanks, Eddie.' She walked to the front door and out into the bright sunlight.

Tony Mifsud lived two suburbs away. It was nearly midday when she got there. The plain-faced brick building stood two stories high, wedged between buildings of equal height. Mifsud's flat was one of four on the upper level. Stephanie climbed the concrete steps and pressed the buzzer. Nothing happened. She wondered if the buzzer was working. She thumped on the wooden door and was relieved to hear footsteps on the other side. The door opened and Stephanie looked into a cold, stony face.

'Are you Tony Mifsud?' Stephanie asked.

'Who wants to know?' The voice was harsh and mocking.

'I'm investigating Jordan Darrieux' murder on the 25th May. I believe you were at the Poplars Arms that night. I'm hoping you might be able to help me.'

'I've told you people everything I know. You won't leave me alone, will you? I get pinned for something five years back and I'm always a suspect.' He slammed the door in her face. Stephanie banged on the door. 'I'm not the police. I'm Jordan's sister,' she yelled.

'Fuck off,' came the muffled reply from the other side.

Stephanie felt defeated and walked back down the stairs. She wondered what Mifsud meant when he talked about being pinned for something five years ago. Did Tony Mifsud have a record? If so, why did Brendan say he was clean?

That night Brendan called for her and they went to the local Chinese restaurant. Brendan was making small talk and Stephanie was having trouble concentrating. She wanted to tell him of her three visits, but something stopped her. Instead, she asked, 'Are you certain Tony Mifsud doesn't have a record?'

'That's what the boss said.' Brendon narrowed his eyes. 'Why do you want to know about Mifsud?'

'Just curious.' Stephanie felt restless during the night. Mifsud's words were still ringing in her ears. She had to know just what he meant by being 'pinned.'

Tom Vaughan would be giving tomorrow's lecture. He might be able to give her the answers she needed.

After the ten o'clock lecture the next day, Stephanie followed Tom Vaughan from the hall. Tom Vaughan was a distinguished lawyer who lectured in criminal law. He was a favourite with the students, mainly because of his marking generosity and his ability to transform dreary lectures into good-natured fun.

'Mr. Vaughan, could I have a minute please?' He turned and smiled as Stephanie approached him.

'Stephanie! How are you doing?' He touched her shoulder lightly. 'You've had a rough time.'

'Yes. It's been rough. I was wondering if you could help me.'

'Of course, I will. I'm impressed with how you've managed to pull it together. I wouldn't have thought you needed any help.' He started walking slowly.

'It's not about my work. It's about the investigation of Jordan's death.' They arrived at Vaughan's rooms. 'Come in'. Tom Vaughan frowned as he opened the door. The room was small with floor-to-ceiling windows running along the length of one wall. A big desk took up half the room. Vaughan waved to a chair.

'Now, what can I do for you?'

'I need to know if a certain person has a criminal record. How do I get this information?'

'This is connected with your brother's murder?'

'Yes.'

'Why don't you just ask the police?'

'The police say the man doesn't have a record. But I have reason to think he might.'

'Why would the police lie?'

'I don't know. I need to satisfy myself. Can you help me get this information?'

'I'll get it for you. Who is this man? I need a name and a description.'

'His name is Tony Mifsud, probably Anthony. He's about thirty, Middle Eastern appearance, short, thin.'

Vaughan took out a notebook and wrote. He looked at Stephanie over his glasses. 'I'll talk to you after

Wednesday's lecture.'

The following Wednesday, Tom Vaughan handed Stephanie a photo. 'Is this your Tony Mifsud?'

Stephanie studied the photo. The cold black eyes glared out at her. 'It is.'

'Well, he *has* got a record. He has served time for procuring and also drug dealing. He's a nasty little man.'

'Why wasn't this brought out at the inquiry? Mifsud was at the pub and Eddie Khoury said he was alone with Jordan during the night. Yet nothing was mentioned of his police record or of Jordan being with him.'

'Take my advice, Stephanie. Let the police do their job.'

'Thanks, Mr. Vaughan, for your help.'

Now Stephanie was in a real quandary. Should she talk to Brendan about all this? She headed home. Sometimes a hot bath gave her answers. On the way to the bathroom, she passed Jordan's room. The door was half opened. She hadn't been in that room since Jordan's death but she knew that Estelle had kept it exactly as it had been when Jordan was alive. She hadn't changed the pillow case or the sheets, or anything else for that matter.

Stephanie knew the police had gone over the room with a fine-tooth comb. They had searched through every drawer, looked in every pocket, and had taken Jordan's computer away for more than a fortnight.

Stephanie felt compelled to enter. She opened the cupboard door. Jordan's things were hanging there just as they always had. She went through the pockets of his trousers, shorts, jackets and shirts, and looked inside his shoes and under his caps.

She didn't know what she was looking for but was sure now that Jordan had a secret and the secret had cost him his life. She moved to his desk and went through the flat boxes that contained the software for his many games. She opened the top drawer and upended a packet of staplers. But something was wrong. The flimsy cardboard box felt too heavy. On closer inspection, she noticed that it had a false bottom. When she pulled it away a small black object tumbled out. Stephanie's eyes widened. It was a flash drive.

She plugged it into the computer. A second later the screen lit up and a single word appeared—'Mifsud.' The screen went blank and then a video started. The camera was focused on a room. It zoomed in on a king-sized bed covered in a red silk spread. A man walked into the picture. He was naked. He moved to the bed and sat on the edge. The camera remained fixed on the bed and the man.

A woman entered the picture. She was tall and slender. Her mahogany-red hair fell to her shoulders. Its colour contrasted sharply with the whiteness of her skin. She was naked except for a leather metal-studded belt hanging around her hips and a matching collar at her throat. Thigh-length stiletto-heeled boots completed the outfit. She carried a small black whip and moved towards the man.

Stephanie noticed her lips moving, but no sounds were coming through. Then the man climbed onto the bed and lay face down. The woman kneeled beside him and started whipping his buttocks.

The man turned over and lay on his back. The woman roughly pulled his hands back and tied them with leather straps dangling from the bedhead. She then tied his feet together with straps at the foot of the bed. The camera zoomed in and focused on the growing penis. Stephanie watched with a mixture of fascination and repulsion. She had never seen an erect penis before.

The woman then climbed on top of the man, positioning herself above the penis. She then slowly sank down on him. She moved over him in a circular fashion and then began an unhurried bounce. The bouncing gradually increased in tempo. All the while, she was whipping the man's thighs and buttocks. Stephanie felt disgusted and fast-forwarded until she saw the woman move off the bed and untie the man's feet and hands. The man sat up and the camera zoomed in on his face. Stephanie drew in her breath. She had seen that man before, but where? Who was he? The girl handed the man his trousers. He pulled out his wallet and counted a large wad of notes into her hand. Then the screen went blank.

Stephanie withdrew the flash drive and turned off the computer. She felt heavy, like stone. Her mind was swirling. *How did Jordan get hold of this filth? What was he doing with it?* It was clear that Tony Mifsud was involved. The video showed his name.

Stephanie felt she now had some evidence she could give the police.

Brendan was doing shift work tonight and would

still be at the station.  She called a taxi and was there in fifteen minutes.

The station was a converted house with a large entry room separated from the main office by opaque glass partitions. Brendan was surprised when he saw her.  She had never been here before.

'What are you doing here?' he asked.

'I've got something to show you.  I think it's a lead to Jordan's murderer.'  As she spoke, a man appeared in the doorway.

'Lloyd, I need you to sort out these papers in the Beckhouse case,' the man said.

'I'll be there in a sec, sir.'  Brendan turned to Stephanie.   At first, he didn't notice her stunned expression.

'I can't keep the Inspector waiting.  Now, what's all this about?' His gaze settled on her face. 'Stephanie, what's wrong?  You look as if you've just seen a ghost!'

'That man—he is your Inspector?   The man handling Jordan's murder?'

'Yes.  He interviewed you the night Jordan was killed.  That's Inspector Manning.  What's wrong?'

'Nothing, I'm sorry, Brendan.  I won't hold you up.' Stephanie turned and almost ran out of the building.  She was in a state of shock. The cold night air filled her lungs and spread to her head.  She felt dizzy and nauseous. Who could she turn to? Who would believe that Inspector Manning was a customer of a prostitute and that prostitute was connected with Tony Mifsud?

Back home, she called Magda and told her the story from beginning to end.

'I don't know what to do.'

'You must give that flash drive to the police.'

'But Manning's in charge of the case.'

'Then you go to someone in charge of Manning.'

The next day Brendan phoned. 'What was all that about last night?'

'Brendan, do you believe that Inspector Manning is an honest cop?'

'I would trust him with my life.'

'What would you say if I told you I have evidence that Manning is involved with a criminal and could be protecting him.'

'I would say you should keep out of police business.' Brendan's tone was harsh and uncompromising.

'You don't want to know about my evidence?'

'I do not. Now, stop trying to act like Miss Marple and get real.'

'Goodbye, Brendan.' Stephanie quietly put the phone down. Tears were brimming in her eyes. Maybe Brendan was not 'Mr Right' after all.

That afternoon she contacted the office of the Minister of Police. The wheels were quickly set in motion and within a short time, both Tony Mifsud and Trevor Manning were arrested.

Brendan called around to Stephanie's house soon after the arrests. He stood awkwardly in the doorway. 'I'm sorry I was so short with you. I looked up to Manning. He was my idol.'

'Come in.' Stephanie led him to the dining room and they sat at the table.

'Mifsud has confessed to drug dealing but not to Jordan's murder,' Brendan murmured.

'Tell me everything. Why was Jordan killed?'

'Jordan was getting his drugs from Mifsud. He got behind with his payments and asked for more time to pay. Mifsud refused. Somehow, Jordan got hold of that flash drive. According to Mifsud, Jordan stole it the last time he was in his flat. It didn't take Jordan long to recognise that the flash drive could cause Mifsud a lot of trouble. So, Jordan threatened to expose the drug dealing, the illegal brothel and the hidden camera if Mifsud didn't wipe his debt and give him a free supply of drugs. It seems that flash drive caused double blackmail. Mifsud had used it against Manning and threatened to release it if Manning didn't protect him and turn a blind eye to his drug dealing...and everything else. Losing that flash drive caused Mifsud one big headache. He was desperate to get it back. Jordan and Mifsud arranged to exchange the flash drive for drugs that night at the hotel. They met in the Men's room. Mifsud swears that Jordan handed the flash drive over and that he gave Jordan a stash of drugs in return. He says he never went anywhere near the lane and reckons that someone bailed Jordan up in the lane, stole the drugs, and knifed him.'

'Do you believe that?'

'No. Mifsud's guilty. We found a knife buried in a pot plant in his flat. It's being tested and we're pretty certain it's the murder weapon. He'll be convicted.'

Stephanie felt some comfort from this but needed to know more. 'Why did Jordan go back?'

'Jordan and Mifsud hadn't finished their business in the Men's room. Eddie Khoury interrupted them. When Jordan heard Mifsud's whistle, he probably thought that Mifsud was going to honour the deal. In the dark lane with no witnesses, Mifsud took the opportunity to grab the flash drive and silence Jordan permanently.'

'But if Mifsud took the flash drive, how did it get back in Jordan's room?'

'Obviously, Jordan made a copy.'

Stephanie slowly digested all this. She was having enormous difficulty coming to terms with Jordan's double life. Brendan broke the silence that was growing between them. 'Manning will face charges of consorting with a criminal and deliberately interfering in the course of justice.' He reached across the table and put his hand on Stephanie's.

'Now, what about dinner tonight?'

'I'm sorry, Brendan, I'm busy.'

'Tomorrow?'

'I've got my final exams coming up soon. I'm not dating you, or anyone else.'

'After the exams?'

'I don't know.'

*

Stephanie sat her final law exams and the results showed she had done extremely well. The Poplars Arms group met that night. Magda hugged her. 'You bright spark. Your results were top of the tree. Congratulations!'

'Thanks, Magda. You didn't do too bad yourself.

Congratulations!'

It was a happy night. Congratulations were sung back and forth across the hotel. They danced and sang and drank a little too much. 'Are you staying on with Smiths?' asked Stephanie.

'I am and I will be looking for a junior partnership before long. Are you staying with Holmes & Holmes?'

'No.'

'Who, then?'

'No one.' Stephanie took a sip of her drink and looked levelly at Magda. 'I've decided against being a lawyer.'

'You're having me on.'

'I've given it a lot of thought these past few weeks. I'm joining the police force.'

# CHAPTER 4
## *Brett - 2022*

The Saturday after Danni's call, I got out of bed with a heavy head. I had scarcely slept a wink the entire night. After hours of lying awake with a brain full of scrambled thinking, I finally came to a decision...I must go to the memorial service today.

During those sleepless hours, my mind had slipped back to the first weeks and months after Crystal's disappearance, to the sadness I felt over losing her, and to my brief brush with insanity.

### 2019

My head seemed to be constantly aching and I was sleeping badly. I told myself this would soon pass. Although shattered by Crystal's disappearance, I was determined to pick up the threads of my life and move on.

Tuesday night came and I set off for tennis around six-thirty. We had a home match so I didn't have far to travel. The team comprised me and Steve and two other guys.

The routine was that we each played two single sets and two doubles. Steve was my partner in one of the doubles and ours was the first set of the night. My legs felt like lead and I couldn't seem to focus on the ball in the warm-up. We won the toss and Steve took the first serve. I had a reputation for being a deadly net player. But tonight, the balls were whizzing past me before I knew they were coming. Steve managed to put in a couple of aces and we won his serve. I lost both my serves badly. We finished six games to two against

'Sorry, mate,' I mumbled as we left the court.

'What happened?' he asked.

'Dunno. I don't seem to be seeing the ball.'

My next three sets were equally bad and I felt lousy and despondent at the end of the night. We lost against a team that we usually wiped off the court. I didn't stay back for a drink and disappeared as quickly as I could.

I fell into bed, not bothering to shower, and was asleep almost instantly. I woke myself up with a strangled scream. My body was shuddering and shaking. I had had a grotesque nightmare. I was on the island again and Crystal was standing near the edge of the cliff. I was walking toward her but didn't see the gaping hole in my pathway. I fell into a cavernous shaft, down to a slimy muddy bottom. There was a corridor cut into the shaft and there was a strong pungent smell, like gas.

Someone was approaching me from the corridor. As the figure came nearer, I saw that it was Hannah

Edwards. She was wearing a white shroud and carried a pillow. Her arms and hands were skeletal. I was terrified. Then I saw other figures coming towards me and I knew they were dead people. I was in a catacomb, there was no way out and I started clawing at the sides of the shaft.

I tried unsuccessfully to dismiss the dream. But its frightening reality triggered anxiety that was crushing and depressing. I got up, made some coffee, and had a hot shower.

As it was now morning, I decided a workout might help, and drove to the gym. Once there, I was seized with a wave of panic. I felt out of place and couldn't bear the thought of doing weights and seeing people.

Back home I fell into bed. The phone rang a few times but I didn't answer it. I lay awake for hours and then drifted off. I was plagued with yet another nightmare. This time I was with Crystal in a rowing boat. We were on the open sea and the water was black and thick like tar. I moved to Crystal, pulled her up, and pushed her overboard into the filthy, black water. I watched her sink. The sleep that followed was fragmented and restless.

A lone bird was calling plaintively and it was dark outside. I felt as if I had been in bed for years and didn't know if it was morning or night. I got up and went to the bathroom. Looking in the mirror I was shocked by the haggard face and glazed red eyes staring at me.

I gradually realised it was morning and my watch told me it was Thursday. I stepped into the shower, turned on the hot tap, and let the water run over me in steaming torrents. Little by little my fuddled brain started to clear and then I remembered today was the beginning of the first university semester and that I was scheduled to give two lectures.

I had offered to be a stand-by lecturer for the first two semesters, as most of my writing was done in the second half of the year. Lecturers were often taking leave or going sick and stand-by lecturers were always in demand. The Dean had quickly taken up my offer and scheduled me for two lectures every Thursday. My first lecture was at ten today.

I dressed carefully and was at the university in good time. I parked my car, crossed the quad, and entered the almost-full lecture hall. Young eager faces looked up at me as I took my place at the lectern. These were first-year students. As I knew the work back to front, I didn't need any notes. I introduced myself and then started with a bit of good-natured banter. A few laughs usually got the kids on side. I then launched into some of the elementary aspects of the course. 'Today we are looking at the safety requirements when handling printed circuit boards and electronic components associated with these boards.'

A boy in the front row suddenly took my attention. I noticed that he was tapping his pen on the desk and reading something that looked like a comic. I felt unduly irritated and couldn't take my eyes off him. I tried to move on and resume my talk.

'The components associated with—.' Suddenly my mind went blank. The tapping pen started sounding like a drum filling my head with its unrelenting beat. The silence in the hall was complete except for the pen. I had to get back to my lecture. But I couldn't remember what I had been saying. I looked at the whiteboard behind me, hoping it might give me a clue. But it was totally blank, just like my mind. I could feel countless eyes on me. My throat was dry and my head was spinning.

'Excuse me.' I mumbled and left the hall. I took out my mobile and was relieved to find that I had recorded the Dean's number. With shaking hands, I punched it in.

'Frank, it's Brett Carlton. I was lecturing but I've had to leave. I'm not well. Can you get someone to take over?'

'There's no one around. I'll go myself. Where are you now?'

'Heading to the car park.'

'You're not going to drive, are you? You should go to the sick bay.'

'I need to get home,' I muttered. I walked out into the sunlight but felt icy cold.

Later, when I tried to recall the journey home, I couldn't remember a single moment of it. On my way to the bedroom, I saw that the answering service light was flashing. There were six messages. I fell into bed fully clothed. I seemed to lose all track of time and fell in and out of sleep.

I thought I heard my mother's voice. I struggled out of bed and padded to the door. My mother stood there. Her eyes opened wide when she saw me.

'Brett!' was all she said as she entered.

'What's wrong?' I mumbled.

'I've left four messages on your phone. You didn't turn up for dinner last night. We've been worried sick. Look at you! You look dreadful! What's happened?'

I scratched my head. Usually, I went to my parent's place for dinner on Wednesdays. Why hadn't I gone? Everything seemed hazy. I had a vague memory of leaving the university, but couldn't remember why.

Mum quickly assessed that I was far from well. She ran a bath for me and started cooking something.

Lying in the warm water, I started feeling incredibly sad. I sank below the surface, thinking it might be a nice peaceful way to escape my misery. I held my breath and my ears started pounding. My lungs felt ready to burst and I broke the surface gasping for air. What in God's name was I thinking of doing?

My parents organised an appointment with a psychiatrist. On their insistence, I reluctantly agreed to keep it.

Two weeks later I sat stiffly in an imposing waiting room. Soft soothing music drifted from unseen speakers. Thick-piled carpet, comfortable leather chairs and modern glass coffee tables created an atmosphere of tranquil prosperity. Expensive works of art graced the walls. I started worrying about the fee.

After a thirty-minute wait, I was ushered into Dr. Attwell's God-like presence. His surgery was as imposing as his waiting room. After scribbling something in a small ledger, he looked at me over his rimless glasses and invited me to tell him why I was there.

He sat with a faraway expression, and at times

I wondered if he was listening.  But at the end of thirty minutes, he had complete knowledge of Crystal's disappearance and the depression that was drowning me.

'I'm going to put you on a course of anti-depressants.  You may find a few side effects to start with, but these will go after a couple of weeks.  I would like to see you again in three weeks.'  He stood, handed me a script, and walked me to the door.

He was right.  The pills had some nasty side effects.  But as my sleeping improved, I decided to keep on with them.

Although I gradually got my life back into some sort of order, I was still caught in the web of depression. I felt I needed to get away to make the final adjustment. I discussed this with the doctor and told him I was thinking of leaving Sydney and moving to Port Stephens.

'Why Port Stephens?'

'It's a beautiful place,' I said simply.

'It could help to get away.  But you should keep on with therapy.'  He scribbled a name on his card and handed it to me.  'Look up Eugene Blackmore.  He's one of the best.'

I called Steve before I left Sydney and told him of my decision.  'Is this permanent?' he asked.

'It depends on how I like it up there.'

'Are you still having...trouble?' he asked hesitantly.

'Trouble?'

'We heard through the grapevine you were seeing a psychiatrist.'

'That's finished…all done and dusted,' I lied.

'Good to hear it. Well then, good luck.'

I was disappointed that he hadn't said anything about keeping in touch or maybe meeting for a drink.

The next week, I headed north and rented a townhouse in Port Stephens.

\*

My first appointment with Eugene Blackmore was a month after I had settled in. His rooms were in a Newcastle suburb. I was surprised to find he practiced from an old free-standing Federation house. His brass plate was on the front fence, so I knew I was at the right place. I parked my car in the narrow street and took the short pathway to the house. A sign on the front door said 'Enter'. Inside, a long narrow hall ran to a closed door. On the right-hand side of the hall was another closed door. On the left were open double glass doors leading to a large room. A desk was set up in a corner and a 'twenty-something' girl sat at a computer. She smiled widely as I approached.

'Brett Carlton to see Dr. Blackmore,' I said.

'Please take a seat. Gene won't be too long.'

I sat on one of the plain upholstered chairs feeling stupidly conspicuous. I was the only one waiting, so why did I feel self-conscious? After a few minutes, I managed to relax and take in my surroundings.

The ceiling was ten feet high with ornate cornices. A few pieces of loose curling plaster told me it had been a while since it had been painted. A marble fireplace was set into a wall. It looked as if it hadn't been used in fifty years. The carpet was grey and a bit worn-looking. I couldn't help comparing this waiting room with that of the Sydney psychiatrist. A patient emerged from the door across the hall and made her way out through the front door.

After a few minutes, the door opened again, and a tall, thin man invited me to enter. The room was small with rows of books stacked against two walls. The man waved me to a chair alongside a large, untidy desk. He sat opposite me and held out his hand. 'Eugene Blackmore,' he said. As we shook hands, I was a bit discomforted by the man's sombre expression. But then he smiled and his face creased into warmth and light. Almost immediately, I felt reassured.

At his prompting, I told Gene the full story of the boat trip, the people on it, Crystal's disappearance, and the aftermath. He looked at me steadily for what seemed an age. Then he spoke. 'No wonder you need help. You've been to hell and back.'

Those words comforted and warmed me. I had received nothing but condemnation and total disregard from people who had been trusted friends. Now a complete stranger was recognising what I had been through and was viewing me with understanding. Gene picked up the referral I had given him.

'I notice here that Dr. Attwell has got you on anti-depressants. Are they helping?'

'They've helped with the insomnia, that's really all. I still feel—' I searched for the word.

'Sad?' He prompted quietly.

'Yes.'

'Well, I want you to get off these pills as soon as you can.'

Gene had me lie on a comfortable couch and, using soothing words, put me into a light hypnotic state. During this time, he made positive suggestions. Afterward, he gave me a set of exercises to do three times each day along with a compact disc. He asked me to come back the following week. I was to keep on with the anti-depressants until he said to stop.

After three months, I was able to cut back the dose and three months after that, stop the pills altogether. I was no longer suffering from panic attacks and my memory had returned. I started writing again, joined the golf club, and even got a part-time lecturing job at Newcastle University. I still had moments of depression and hoped that in time these would disappear.

*

Those memories had contributed to my restless night and I felt totally drained as I prepared for the trip to Sydney.

Driving through the peaceful countryside of Port Stephens, I allowed myself to restore more buried memories. Should I reveal today what I knew about Crystal? Would it make any difference? Maybe not, but I couldn't help thinking it was a stroke of fate that I had uncovered a secret.

It had happened one Saturday afternoon after golf, nearly two years after Crystal's disappearance. I had been living in Port Stephens for about eighteen months. One of my golfing mates invited me around to his house for dinner.

Doug was a lot older than me but we enjoyed each other's company, both on the course and later, at the 'nineteenth tee'. Doug's wife Gail was a long-suffering 'golf widow' but welcomed me with genuine affection.

We sat in the cool family room and sipped our drinks while Gail pottered in the kitchen. Long glass windows looked out onto a thickly planted tropical garden.

'Do you have kids?' I asked.

'Yes three...two boys and a girl. Ian and Andrew are both overseas at present and our daughter lives in Sydney. She has given us two lovely grandkids.' Doug picked up a photo from a nearby coffee table. 'This is Fiona with her two girls.' He handed me the photo. 'Very nice,' I said as I appraised the pleasant-looking girl with her two pretty kids.

'She was a champion swimmer you know,' said Doug proudly.

'Oh?'

'Yes, when she was in high school. She was State Junior Champion at fifteen. But she lost the title the next year.' Doug took the photo and replaced it on the table. He opened the drawer below and brought out a magazine. He sorted through the pages and handed the opened magazine to me. 'There she is getting her medal'. The photo showed a younger, thinner version of Fiona receiving a medal. Doug rifled through another magazine. 'There she is again the following year, this time the runner-up. That girl beat her by two seconds.'

Doug pointed to a coloured photo of another girl receiving her medal.

I froze, as I stared at the photo and read the caption beneath. *The Junior State Swimming Champion: Crystal Morgan.*

Doug must have sensed my shock. 'What's up?'

'I knew Crystal Morgan,' I murmured.

'Fancy that!'

Gail appeared in the doorway. 'Dinner's ready. Come and get it.'

I went home that night, puzzled. *Why had Crystal told everyone she couldn't swim?*

# CHAPTER 5
## *Brett- 2022*

All those memories charged me emotionally as I drove to Sydney, and I was agitated and nervous by the time I reached my destination.

Although it was still only early December, the steadily rising temperatures were promising a hot summer. I spotted the group gathered beneath a big oak in the centre of the park. Shelly looked straight ahead, avoiding my gaze. She was standing with a short stocky man who I guessed was Lance Gibson. Danni smiled faintly and invited me with a hand gesture to come closer. None of them had changed much although Rick was looking older and thinner. Jaz was the only one who had improved. Her dark straight hair was now a light blonde and she seemed to have put on a few pleasant curves. Nearby, but apart from the group, stood a tall slim woman and a tall skinny man. I decided that these two were police. Jaz threw me a little wave and Steve gave me the 'thumbs up.'

A middle-aged woman looked at me with raised eyebrows. 'You must be Mr. Carlton.' I nodded.

'Well, we're all here now and we can begin.' She walked to a spot that gave her a height advantage over all of us. I decided she must be a celebrant of some sort. She flicked through some papers and then looked at us with a well-rehearsed sad smile. 'We are here today to celebrate the life of our dear friend Crystal. At last, she has been found and at last, we can acknowledge and mourn her passing.'

The woman went on to talk about Crystal's life as if she knew her. I thought it was all a load of crap. The woman knew nothing about Crystal, nothing about her life or her death—that is if Crystal *was* dead!

The celebrant then invited Jaz to say a few words. Jaz moved to the front of the group and spoke shakily. 'Crystal was our dear friend. She was a lovely girl, quiet...a little shy. She had a great future ahead of her as a graphic designer and she gave one hundred percent to her job. I never heard Crystal say a bad word about anybody. She was a good person. She had a cruel start in life and an even worse end. She was much too young to die. What she went through, we will probably never know. We can only hope she didn't suffer too much. We were with her on her last days and I think none of us will be able to resume normal lives until we know exactly what happened to her.' A little tear trickled down Jaz's cheek as she moved back to Steve's side.

The celebrant took this as her cue to continue her 'program'. She moved back to her spot and smiled sadly. 'We say goodbye to Crystal knowing that we will always hold her close to our hearts.' The woman's eyes scanned the group. 'I understand Crystal had a belief in the afterlife, and accordingly, I will now recite a short prayer for the repose of her soul.' The woman said the Lord's Prayer. Everyone said '*Amen*' at the end.

Danni came over to me. 'We're having a few drinks at our place.'

The two people I assumed were police, joined us. 'This is Detective Darrieux. She will be coming back to the house. She wants to talk to us all,' said Danni.

'I'm sorry. I won't be coming,' I said, staring into space and avoiding Danni's gaze.

'We have positive confirmation that we are investigating a murder. Everyone who was on that boat that night will be required to give a statement. It would be of great assistance to us if you joined the others at Mrs. Melville's house—today,' said Darrieux.

Steve, Ben and Jaz came over. I shook hands with the guys and Jaz pecked me on the cheek. There was an air of solemnity around the occasion and the atmosphere was like a funeral...but one without a corpse.

It seemed I had no choice but to go back to Danni's place. I followed the cars and we all arrived together.

Ben brought out drinks. Steve came over and sat next to me. 'How's it going, mate?' he asked.

'Okay, *mate*.' I emphasised the 'mate'. I was still stinging from the way they had all dumped me.

Detective Darrieux arrived soon after. She refused a drink and removed her oversized sunglasses. I noticed her eyes were a startling green. Appraising the rest of her, I decided she was quite attractive.

She moved to the centre of the room and slowly shifted her gaze from face to face.

'Thank you all for coming here today. I am Detective Sergeant Stephanie Darrieux and this is Detective Constable Phillip Lockwood.' She waved her hand in Lockwood's direction. 'The body we found last week had sustained a sizeable blow to the back of the head. The pathologist has ascertained that this was the cause of death.' Darrieux stopped and looked around the group, observing each person's reaction. 'You all gave statements at the time of Crystal Morgan's disappearance and I have them in my file.' She held up a bulging file. 'I will interview each of you privately again, but today I want to hear what you have to say as a group. Most of my questions will be the same as those you answered back in 2019.' Darrieux opened the file and withdrew a bundle of pages stapled together. She studied the top page for a few seconds, and then cast a long hard stare in Rick Bradshaw's direction.

'Mr Bradshaw, you were Crystal's partner and you were sleeping with her in one of the cabins the night she disappeared.'

'That's right,' said Bradshaw.

'When did you first know Crystal was missing?'

'Around seven the next morning. She wasn't in bed. At first, I wasn't worried. She usually got up before me. But pretty soon I knew she wasn't on board.'

'You looked for her in the water and then called Marine Rescue. Is that right?'

'Steve called Marine Rescue.'

Darrieux's eyes continued to include each one of

us as she spoke. 'You probably all know that the dinghy was found some distance downstream. There was no sign of foul play and the oars were still intact. The coroner concluded that Crystal was missing, presumed dead.'

There was a short silence as I, and I guess the others, were recalling the harrowing events of that morning.

Darrieux continued. 'Was there anything leading up to Crystal's disappearance that you might tell me about?' There was an uncomfortable silence as Darrieux bored Bradshaw with her gaze.

'I dunno. We all drank a lot. I didn't know any of them much. They were Crystal's friends.'

Darrieux looked at her file. 'I have it here that Jacinta Rochford saw you throw Crystal's diary overboard. What made you do that?'

'I was so upset at the time. I didn't know what I was doing.'

'Rather an unusual action for someone who had just lost a loved one?'

Bradshaw just hung his head and said nothing.

'How long had you known Crystal?'

'Eighteen months, maybe a bit longer.'

Darrieux pursed her lips. "What sort of a person was Crystal?'

'Very beautiful, but insecure.'

'Why was she insecure?'

'Something to do with her past. She was adopted.'

Darrieux seemed to be considering this and then

spoke again. 'You were a great deal older than her?'

'Yes.'

'It must have been something of a triumph for you to get a beautiful young girl to move in and share your life.'

'I resent that.'

'Sorry.' Darrieux knew she had broken certain boundaries, but unperturbed, she carried on. 'So besides being insecure, what else can you tell me about Crystal?'

'She liked nice things. She was a spender.'

'That's all?'

'Yes.'

'How did you meet her?'

'In the lift. She worked on the floor below me. We talked in the lift and then I asked her out for a coffee.'

'And?' prompted Darrieux

'And then we had a few dinners together and I asked her to move in with me.'

'And she did?'

'Yes, I loved her.'

'And she loved you?'

'Yes.'

'What did she bring with her, to your place?'

'She was renting a furnished flat. She only brought her clothes and personal things.'

Is that all? No car?'

'No, she didn't have a car. Just her personal things—and a coffee maker.'

'She brought a coffee maker with her?'

'Yes, that's all.'

'What happened when Crystal remained missing? What did you do?'

'I tried to get on with my life, but that was hard because the cops—the police kept coming to my place asking questions and checking through her things.'

'And you still have her things?'

'I gave her clothes and shoes to charity. It depressed me to look at them every day.'

'And what about her personal things?'

'I threw away her make-up and all that stuff. I kept the coffee maker.'

'You kept the coffee maker?'

'It made good coffee.'

'What about her money? She had a bank account, I presume?'

'There were only a few dollars in her bank account.'

'But she worked?'

'Yes, but she spent. All those clothes were very expensive.'

Darrieux turned her attention to me. 'Mr Carlton. I have it here in these notes that on the last day of the cruise, you and Crystal were missing from the group for a substantial length of time. Could you tell me what happened between you?'

'I don't know what you mean.'

'I mean, what happened?'

'Nothing happened.'

Darrieux smiled tightly. She glanced at the bundle and turned a couple of pages. She then looked up and fixed me with a steady gaze.

'You said you saw a big cruiser each night you were on the river. You thought it was the same boat.'

'I can't be sure it was the same cruiser. It was anchored a fair distance away. But there was a full moon on each of the nights.' The vision of the big sleek cruiser gleaming in the moonlight came readily to my mind.

'And?' prompted Darrieux.

'I did look at it through binoculars once, but I can't be sure it was the same boat.'

'Anything else you want to tell me?'

'Yes, two things. Crystal made calls on her mobile during the cruise. Twice I saw her. I got the feeling both times she was being a bit secretive about it.'

'Could you hear what she was saying during either of these calls?'

'Only the last time. It was something like: 'Don't worry, I'll be okay.' I brushed my hand through my hair. 'It was a long time ago.'

'Why didn't you mention these calls in your early statement?'

'I didn't think they were important, at the time.'

Darrieux turned another page before addressing Bradshaw.

'Mr Bradshaw, have you any idea what these calls were about?' asked Darrieux.

'No.' Bradshaw's face was impassive.

'Anyone else heard or saw Crystal talking on her mobile?'

I looked around the room. They were all shaking their heads.

'You said there were two things, Mr Carlton. What was the other thing?'

'Crystal told everyone she couldn't swim. Recently I saw an article in an old sporting journal. Crystal Morgan was a state junior swimming champion when she was sixteen.'

I could see from their expressions this was news to everyone. 'I'm surprised the police hadn't picked it up when they were investigating,' I added.

Darrieux ignored this and directed her next question to Bradshaw. 'Why do you think Crystal wanted everyone to believe she couldn't swim?'

Bradshaw rolled his eyes and shrugged. 'She told me she couldn't swim and I believed her.'

'Anyone else know why Crystal Morgan didn't want people to think she couldn't swim?'

Darrieux looked from one to another of us.

'Haven't a clue,' said Jaz. Darrieux turned her attention to Jaz. 'Ms Rochford, you probably knew Crystal longer than anyone in the group.'

'I hadn't known her very long.' Jaz bit her lip and frowned.

'But you worked with her. What sort of person was she?'

'Just what I said at the service. She was quiet, a bit shy. But I don't think I really got to know her.'

'You invited her to your home. I have it here on file.'

'Yes, but now I come to think of it, she sort of invited herself. She had overheard me on the phone talking to Danni. I was inviting Danni and Ben over for a party. I remember telling Danni I was making it a big party because it was Steve's birthday. When I got off the phone Crystal dropped so many hints about coming too, I had to invite her.'

'So, no one knew much about Crystal,' Darrieux murmured almost to herself. She swung her attention to Shelly. 'Can you add anything that might help this investigation, Mrs Gibson?'

I looked at Shelly. She was sitting close to Gibson. He had a protective arm around her shoulder. 'Crystal Morgan was a scheming bitch. She set out to get Brett, and she succeeded.' Shelly looked accusingly at me and hissed. 'I saw them. I saw them together. He was on top of her. He betrayed me.'

So, Shelly *had* seen us. How could she have not said anything? How could she have returned to the beach, sat in the cruiser, and not said anything? Then I remembered seeing Shelly and Crystal talking when I returned to the beach. I felt certain that Crystal wouldn't have said anything about what had happened between us. I started thinking about the diary. It didn't ring true that Crystal had written about us in her diary and just left it around for Rick to find. Shelly had seen me with Crystal and she must have told Rick. Rick made up the story about reading it in the diary. But why? And why had he thrown the diary overboard?

Darrieux looked at me as she spoke. 'I don't know that any of what you've just said helps this investigation, Ms Gibson. What have you to say about all that, Mr Carlton?' Darrieux bore into me with those brilliant green eyes.

'I have nothing to say,' I said quietly.

Rick looked flustered. His face had lost all colour. The others just sat there with grim expressions.

Then Steve, who had been deadly quiet for the entire time, spoke. 'Are you saying, Detective, that one of us bopped Crystal on the head, somehow got her to that island, and buried her?'

'I'm not making any accusations. But there's been a homicide and you people, whether you like it or not, are involved.'

'Why do you think the body is Crystal Morgan's?' It was Ben talking.

'The body was found in a location not far from where your boat had anchored. The time frame fits as does the physical description. Also, the bracelet found on the left wrist was identified by Mrs Melville,' said Darrieux.

Those words set up alarm bells. 'Did you say the bracelet was on the *left* wrist?' I asked.

'Yes.'

'Then it's not Crystal. She was not wearing a bracelet on her left wrist that day.' My mind had transported me back to that delicious moment in time. I saw her hand in mine as I lifted it to my lips and kissed it. I could still see the long-tapered ring-less fingers and the bare wrist. There was no doubt. There was no bracelet on her left hand.

'How do you know?' asked Darrieux.

'I know.'

'What about dental records?' asked Steve.

'Crystal doesn't appear to have had a regular dentist and no one has come forward yet with any records.'

'She had beautiful teeth,' said Danni.

'There was very little dental work done on the victim,' said Darrieux.

'The place where this body was found, it was an island?' I asked.

'A very tiny island, not much more than a clump of scrubby bushes fringed by sand.' Darrieux flicked through her file. 'This is an aerial photo of the island.' She held up a coloured photo.

'May I?'

She handed me the photo. The little island was marked with an 'x'. I could picture our boat anchored near Dead Man's Island. I could also picture the mysterious cruiser. The little island was close to its anchorage.

'The cruiser I saw that night, was anchored near that island,' I said. Darrieux threw me an interested look.

'Who found the body?' asked Steve.

'It's a miracle it was found. People rarely visit that tiny patch. These were day trippers and they had a dog with them. He started sniffing and digging. It was a shallow grave.'

'Was her mobile found?' Jaz asked.

'No,' said Darrieux, shaking her head. She walked to the window and turned to face us. 'Is there anything at all that any of you can add that might help?'

There was no reply. Darrieux collected her bag

and slipped on her sunglasses. 'I'll be contacting each of you. Please don't leave town. Oh, Mr. Carlton, do I have your Sydney address?'

I had decided to stay with my folks for a few days. they were still living in the old house up at Newport. I pulled out my card and handed it to her. 'You can contact me on my mobile.'

Danni showed the two police officers to the door. Ben refilled my glass. Shelly stood. 'We'll be off too.' She and Gibson left without a goodbye to anyone.

'Was Shelly telling the truth?' asked Jaz.

'What about?' I knew what was coming.

'About you and Crystal on the island.'

'You believed her before.'

'I don't know what to think. None of us do.'

'You judged me three years ago and came back with a verdict of 'guilty'. What's changed?'

Danni looked into her hands. I knew my words were abrasive. But hell, I hadn't deserved their unfair judgment.

Danni found her voice. 'Shelly's changed, she's cold and distant. And we thought Crystal had committed suicide.'

'And you blamed me for that?' I said taking a mouthful of beer. Suddenly it tasted sour. I put down the glass and stood. 'You blamed me.' I walked to the door.

# CHAPTER 6
## *Brett*

I had intended to stay a few days in Sydney. It seemed now that it would be longer. Going back home and being with my parents again was revisiting a happy past, a past that held no pain and no sorrow. The house commanded magnificent views of the ocean and was close to the beach. I felt almost like a happy, carefree kid again.

My old pushbike was still in the garage and the next morning I pedalled down to the beach. Catching a wave still carried the same thrill for me as it had the first time. I mastered that when I was nine. I had intended to do some research while in Sydney and had brought my laptop and my notes. But I couldn't seem to get enough enthusiasm to make a start. Maybe tomorrow, I promised myself.

Three days passed and then Darrieux phoned me. 'I'm trying to build up a profile of Crystal Morgan and get a better picture of what happened the night she disappeared. I've made arrangements for the other parties to come in for private interviews. Is it possible for you to come into police headquarters sometime soon?'

I felt I had no option but to agree to see Darrieux.

Also, I needed desperately to know what had happened to Crystal.

'Okay, I'll come,' I said.

'Good. Would Friday at eleven suit you?'

'That's fine.'

She gave me the address and suggested I use the station's underground parking.

*

Stephanie Darrieux greeted me in the foyer of Sydney's police headquarters and led me to her office. Today she was wearing a short cream skirt set off by a fuchsia-pink shirt.

'Thank you for coming. I've spoken to the Rochfords, the Gibsons and the Melvilles. Mr Bradshaw's coming in this afternoon.'

Stephanie Darrieux waved me to a chair and sat opposite at her desk. 'It was probably a bit unusual for me to talk to you all together the other day. But sometimes memories can be jogged by others.' She smiled faintly as she opened a file and gave it her attention. 'You said you had only met Crystal Morgan on two occasions prior to the boat trip?' Her eyes moved from the opened page and levelled with mine.

'That's right.'

'And the same for Rick Bradshaw?'

'Yes.'

'You were alone with Crystal that last day on the island.' I felt this was a statement rather than a question and said nothing.

'Mrs Gibson said she saw you with Crystal.'

'Mrs Gibson was in a highly emotional state that

day.  I believe it's her word against mine.'

Darrieux raised her eyebrows.  'Why would she make this accusation against you, if it wasn't true?'
I shrugged my shoulders and remained silent.

She returned her attention to the file.  'Is there anything else you can remember that might help the investigation?'

'Only the noise I heard during the night.'

'Oh yes.  You mentioned that in your first statement.  Tell me about it.'

'It was a sort of bumping noise against the boat.'

'Could it have been someone falling overboard?'

'I think it was more like something solid knocking against the side. '

'Why didn't you investigate at the time?'

'My legs felt like lead.  I fell back to sleep almost straight away.'

Darrieux shifted in her chair.  'Funny you should say that.  When I looked at the first report, it stated that everyone on board claimed they had slept unusually soundly that night.  I'm wondering if you could have been drugged.'

The idea seemed preposterous to me.  I shook my head in disbelief.  Stephanie Darrieux continued.  'What did you all eat and drink that night?'

I searched my memory.  'We had a barbeque lunch but I don't remember what we had for dinner.  I can't possibly remember what I ate or what anyone else ate.  I think we might have just had nibbles that night.  But I do remember we all had coffee. I remember that, because someone spilled their coffee all over the table, and there was a commotion because that was where Steve and Jaz were going to bunk'.

'Who made the coffee?'

'Shit Stephanie, it was three years ago.'

'Do you remember who spilled their coffee?'

'No,' I said flatly. Darrieux seemed to accept this before continuing. 'I've been trying to find out more about our mysterious Crystal. I looked up her previous address. She had lived on and off with her parents in Mona Vale. They both died the year before she disappeared.'

'I know.'

Darrieux raised her eyebrows in a question.

'She told me.'

'Did you also know that Crystal spent a year or so in juvenile detention?'

This news started an annoying pulse to throb in my temple. 'No,' I said hoarsely.

'Crystal was on a drug charge when she was seventeen. She and another girl were dealing at school. Last week I visited the convent she attended and spoke to the principal. She told me that Crystal was found with drugs and had been charged with selling them to other students.'

I whistled. 'What kind of drugs?'

'A type of amphetamine.' Darrieux eyed me slowly before she spoke again. 'Was Crystal taking drugs on the occasions you saw her?'

'No, I don't think so. If she was, it wasn't obvious.'

'On the boat, were you or any of the others taking drugs?''

'We were into alcohol. That was our scene, but Crystal and Rick...I don't know about them. How come you people are just coming up with this information about Crystal now?' I asked.

'We knew at the time of her disappearance that Crystal Morgan had a record.'

A uniformed man appeared at the doorway. 'Got a minute, Stephanie?'

'Excuse me.' She quickly rose and left the room. In the next second, I made a decision and grabbed the open file. When I heard her returning footsteps, I carefully replaced it.

Darrieux sat opposite me again. 'Sorry for that,' she said. She looked at the file again and then focused on me with her amazing eyes. 'What do you think happened to Crystal Morgan?' The question took me by surprise.

'I don't think she's dead.' I whispered.

Why don't you?'

'I just don't. What's going to happen now?' I asked.

'We haven't been able to make a positive identification of the body but everything points to it being Crystal Morgan.'

'What about DNA tests using hairbrushes, toothbrushes...all that stuff.'

'We have nothing of Crystal's that can provide us with that type of testing. Apparently, Mr Bradshaw disposed of all her things soon after the incident.'

'Don't you think that's a bit suspicious?'

Darrieux fixed me with a silent stare. Her face

was impassive.  After a few seconds, she spoke:

'I noticed on your card you live up the coast. Could you write down your Sydney address?'

She handed me a card and pen. I wrote down my parent's address.  Darrieux stood and ushered me out of her office.

My peek at Darrieux's file had given me the name of Crystal's school.  I decided I should find out just exactly what happened there all those years ago.

*

The convent was situated in the beachside suburb of Narrabeen.  It was a huge stone building spread over a large parcel of land.  I parked my car in the street and walked through the tall wrought-iron gates. I entered the building through an open doorway and made my way to the small office at the far end of the foyer. Here I was greeted by a smiling, middle-aged woman.

'Could I see the principal, please?' I asked.

'Do you have an appointment?'

'No, I don't.'

'I'm sorry but you must have an appointment if you wish to see Sister Monica.  She's very busy, you know.'

'I'm investigating a murder.  A girl who was a previous student went missing three years ago.  A body has been found and we're trying to establish whether or not it is Crystal Morgan.'

'Oh yes, two detectives were here last week. I'll see if Sister can see you.'  She picked up the phone and pressed some buttons. 'Sister, a gentleman from the police is here. It's about Crystal Morgan. Might you have time to talk to him?'

The receptionist had obviously assumed I was a policeman. I decided against correcting her. She turned to me. 'Sister will see you. Go down the hall and take the first turn on your left. Sister's office is right there.'

'Thank you.' I walked down the hallway feeling a bit guilty for my deception. A strong smell of polish filled my nostrils. Dappled light from the high windows sketched pale patterns along the gleaming floorboards. I arrived at the office and knocked on the door.

'Come in,' called a soft female voice.

Sister Monica was a well-built woman with curly grey hair and pale blue eyes. She wore a pink linen dress with a shirt collar and short sleeves. I was relieved to be talking to a modern-day nun rather than one in the medieval robes of yesteryear. She sat behind a huge oak desk and waved me to a seat opposite her.

'Thank you for seeing me, Sister.'

'I'm afraid I'm in the middle of something quite important and can only give you fifteen minutes.' She smiled apologetically.

'My name is Brett Carlton. I am investigating Crystal Morgan's disappearance. A body has been found and it's thought it could be hers.'

'Yes, the two detectives that came here last week told me all that.'

'I need to know more about the drug incident. What can you tell me?'

'Only what I told the other two police. Crystal was in Year Eleven. A large supply of drugs was found in

her locker.  Crystal denied knowing they were
drugs.  She blamed the other girl as the drug dealer.'

'Could you tell me about the other girl?'

'Rachael Livingstone.  Rachael was in Year
Twelve she was nearly two years older than Crystal.
Rachel put the blame on Crystal.  She said Crystal had
approached her and asked her if she wanted to earn
some money.  The deal was that Rachael would meet
various students after school, give them a package, and
collect money.  Rachael claimed that she had no idea
the packages contained drugs.  She said Crystal had told
her they were discount cosmetics.  She said that for
every packet she handed out, Crystal gave her two
dollars.'

'And Crystal's story?'

She said that Rachael had told her the packages
contained cosmetics and that Rachael wanted to use her
locker because hers was too full.  She even had a key
cut so that she could use Crystal's locker any time she
wanted to.  Crystal said that Rachael was constantly
coming to her locker putting packages in and taking them
out.'

'If that's true, why did Crystal allow it?  Were they
special friends?'

'Far from it.  Rachael had apparently bullied
Crystal over the years.  Crystal said she was too afraid
to say 'no' to Rachael.'

'Do you know why Rachael bullied Crystal?'

'I think she might have been jealous.  Crystal was
very pretty and Rachael was rather plain.  I have their
class photos.  They were taken just before the problem.'

crystal

Sister Monica took out a thin folder from her drawer. She handed me a photo. It was black and white and a bit grainy. She got up from her desk and stood behind me. Leaning over my shoulder, she pointed, 'That's Crystal.' I looked at the photo. It was Crystal all right. Her pretty, smiling face leaped out at me and gave my insides a jolt. Monica dropped another photo on top of the first. 'And that's Rachael,' said Sister Monica pointing to a tall girl standing in the back row. The girl was exceptionally plain. Her chin was receded and her nose was big and bumpy. Her long straight hair fell limply around her shoulders and she wore dark-rimmed glasses.

'Looks won't matter when we're in God's kingdom, Mr Carlton, but unfortunately on this earth, they carry a lot of weight,' said Monica sadly.

'Do you have any opinion as to who was telling the truth?' I asked.

'I can only say that Crystal Morgan was a good student. She was quiet but insecure, and never gave any trouble. On the other hand, Rachael was often in trouble for truancy, and not an easy girl to control. She was quite bright and had an excellent memory. She could have done well but she obviously chose not to.'

'Why was Crystal insecure?' I asked this even though I knew the answer.

'I think it had something to do with her background. She was an abandoned baby. Her adoptive parents were a lot older than the other parents. I really don't know.'

'And Rachael's background?'

'She came from a rather dysfunctional family. We don't know much about her father but we do know that her mother had some sort of mental illness.'

Monica walked to a nearby window and looked out. She sighed heavily. 'You know, Mr Carlton, it's very difficult teaching adolescents today. Values are different from the old-fashioned ones. Young people have too many choices, too many distractions. I've been teaching for nearly fifty years and it gets harder every year.'

'How was the drug trading discovered?' I asked.

'A Year Twelve student came forward. She confessed to being a purchaser but she refused to name any other users. Obviously, she was protecting her fellow students. She claimed it was always Rachael who gave her the packages and took the money.'

'What happened to Crystal and Rachael?'

'They were both found guilty and sent to juvenile detention centres…different centres, I believe.'

'And you have never heard of them since?'

'No, but I learned that Rachael's mother died while Rachael was in detention.' Sister Monica looked at her watch. 'I'm so sorry, Mr Carlton. I must get back to my students.'

'Thank you for your time, Sister.'

I walked slowly back to my car. I couldn't get the image of Crystal's smiling young face out of my mind. I put the car in motion and was stunned to feel tears running down my cheeks. A sob rose from deep in my gut area and I pulled over to the kerb. My body started shaking with sobs. I had never cried for Crystal. I had tried hard to forget her, but seeing her again seemed to tap into grief that was all-consuming and, in a small way, cathartic. After what seemed like an eternity, I pulled myself together. Grieving was important, and maybe now, I had entered the final road to recovery. But I knew that total closure wouldn't come until I found out exactly what had happened to Crystal. There and then, I decided that I would make this happen.

I took out my mobile and called Danni and Steve's number. Danni answered. 'Hey Brett.' Her tone was bright and friendly. 'Danni, I've been to see Detective Darrieux.'

'Yes. We've been too, but we had nothing new to tell her.'

'Nor did I.'

'I'm glad you called, Brett. I'm sorry things turned out the way they did. We took Shelly's side and I guess that was a bit unfair. We've both missed you.'

'Thanks, Danni. I appreciate that. But talking of Shelly, do you know where she went, after she left me?'

'It wasn't long before she moved in with Lance Gibson.'

Do you have her address?' I asked.

Danni gave it to me. I parked outside the massive waterfront home in the exclusive suburb of Church Point. Double wrought-iron gates barred entry to the property. A brick driveway wound its way around a well-manicured lawn.

In the middle was a pond complete with statues and a fountain. Shrubs and trees partly hid the two-level house which spread across the entire block. A four-car garage was open and I saw a Mercedes Benz parked outside. I wondered how and when Shelly had met this Mr. Big. Well, the girl had what she always wanted—a big house and a Mercedes.

The following day I rode my bike down to the beach. I had a quick swim and was pedalling back, when I saw Stephanie Darrieux and Lockwood walking up the path to the front door of the house. 'That's good timing,' smiled Stephanie. I opened the door and we all trooped inside.

'Come through.' I led them to the family room and waved to some chairs but they both remained standing.

'We've just come from the Gibson's. I wanted to ask Mrs Gibson a few more questions. It appears that she was with Rick Bradshaw when he threw Crystal's diary overboard.'

'And?'

'She didn't have anything to add.'

'Why do you put so much importance on the diary?'

'Crystal Morgan recorded everything in her diary. Bradshaw disposed of it. Why?' Stephanie searched my face with her lovely eyes.

'So, you think Bradshaw didn't give the real reason why he threw it overboard?'

Darrieux remained silent.

'If you think Bradshaw's got something to hide, why don't you get a warrant to search his place?' I asked.

'We don't have enough grounds to get a warrant.'

'Can't you make grounds?'

'Don't be silly.'

'Did you go inside Shelly's house?'

'Yes.'

'What's it like?'

'Opulent.'

'Do you know how Gibson makes his money?'

'Apparently, he's in the importing business.' There was a brief silence and she spoke again. 'You gave the impression that you thought Crystal was still alive. Do you still think this?'

'I don't know what to think.'

'Why did you leave Sydney?'

'I'd lost my girlfriend, lost my friends, why not?' I didn't want Darrieux to know that I had suffered a breakdown.

'A big step.'

'As a freelance writer, it doesn't matter much where you live.'

'How long are you staying here?'

'I'll probably stay another week.'

'Good, I might need to talk to you again.'

'What do you plan to do next, or is that privileged information?'

'I'm afraid we have come to a bit of a blank wall. It's an intriguing case. The divers did a thorough search around the boat soon after Crystal went missing. The body was found three years later, some distance away— buried. How did it get there? The dinghy was found in the opposite direction.'

Stephanie Darrieux walked toward the front door. I beat her to it and opened it. We walked out onto the deck. Lockwood bounded down the stairs in front of us. Darrieux stood gazing out at the sea.

'That water looks delicious,' she murmured. 'Do you surf?' she asked.

'I do indeed, mostly body surfing.'

'My aunt lives not far from here. I'll probably spend some time with her over the Christmas break. I might see you on the beach,' she said as she started down the stairs. She stopped halfway down and turned. 'By the way, I wonder if you could arrange for me to look over the cruiser you hired. I need to get an idea of where everyone was that night.'

'Okay, I'll call Jaz. She knows the owner.'

'Thanks.' She threw the word back without turning her head.

I sat thinking for a long while. Stephanie Darrieux obviously had her suspicions about Rick Bradshaw. Yet she couldn't get a warrant. A plan started buzzing in my head. I picked up the phone. Jaz answered. 'Hi, Jaz, how's it going?' I tried to sound cheerful.

'Fine, Brett. We want you to come over for drinks. What are you up to?'

'Pretty free, but first I need two things. Darrieux wants to look at the cruiser we hired. Do you think you can organise that with the owner?'

'I don't see why not. I'll call him.'

'Good girl. Now, do you have Crystal's old address?'

'Yes, why do you want that?'

'Darrieux wants it.'

'I'm surprised Darrieux doesn't have it.'

'Is Rick still living there?'

'Of course. It's his house.'

'So it is.'

There was a short silence and Jaz came back with the address. 'What about making it Christmas Eve for drinks? Are you free then?'

'Sure am.'

Jaz phoned me back later saying that the owner of the cruiser was okay about Darrieux going aboard. It was anchored at the marina and the keys were with the manager. I relayed this to Darrieux.

'Do you mind meeting me there? I'll need someone to tell me where you all slept that last night.' I agreed to meet her the following day.

*

Stephanie was already in the manager's office when I arrived. We collected the keys and wandered down the jetty to the anchored cruiser. The sunlight dancing on the water was dazzling. I was grateful for my sunnies.

We came to the boat and Stephanie lithely jumped on board. I stood for a moment as emotions flooded me. This was the first time I had seen the boat since that terrible day. I shook off the memories and jumped. We entered the main cabin.

'Now tell me where everybody slept that last night,' Stephanie prompted.

'I stepped down to the cabins and pulled aside the curtains.

'Crystal and Bradshaw had this one and Steve and Jaz had that one.

I hopped up the stairs and pointed to the lounge chairs.

'I was on that bunk and Shelly was on that one.'

'Could you set up the lounges and the table ready for sleeping?' Stephanie asked.

It took me a few minutes to convert the table and side lounges.

Darrieux walked around silently. 'So, when you woke up in the middle of the night, it was too dark for you to know if anyone was missing from their bed?'

Yes, the curtains were all drawn and it was very dark inside the cabin.'

Stephanie nodded thoughtfully. 'Thanks for coming, Brett. This has been useful.'

We walked slowly back to the car park. 'What does Rick Bradshaw do these days?' I asked casually.

I believe he's a night watchman at the docks.'

'I thought he worked in an advertising office in the city.'

'He used to, but he wanted a change—or so he told me.'

I walked Stephanie to her car and then headed home. I made a few phone calls and established that Rick Bradshaw worked night shifts at the city docks.

After dinner, I dressed in my black track pants, black hoodie and black sneakers and headed out to Mona Vale. I drove slowly past Bradshaw's house and noted a light still on in an upstairs room. I parked around the corner, walked back, and stood opposite the house, watching. My hand brushed against the small hammer and torch in my pocket.

The upstairs light went out and a minute later the garage door opened. Rick Bradshaw's car reversed into the street and drove off. I waited a few minutes, crossed the road, and walked down the side path to the back of the house. I tried the back door but it was locked. All the windows were quite small and well off the ground. On the back wall was a section of glass panels with a locked sliding glass door in the centre. I took out my hammer and smashed the glass near the keyhole. I put my hand inside, found the lock, released it, slid the door aside, and entered a dark room. I played my torch around and saw a leather lounge suite arranged around a coffee table. A television set was mounted on the opposite wall. There were no bookcases or cupboards and the walls were bare of pictures. Running off this room was a small dining room containing a teak dining table and six chairs. The adjoining kitchen was small and confined. I pulled open drawers and cupboards and found nothing of interest. Nearby was a door that opened into the empty garage. I headed back to the living room and the staircase.

At the top of the stairs were three bedrooms and a bathroom. There was nothing in the bathroom apart from the usual stuff: shaving gear, toothpaste, soap, medical creams and innocuous-looking tablets. I went to the bedroom facing the street.

A queen bed covered in a black and white silky quilt took up most of the room. Next to it was a small bedside table. The top drawer contained some loose change, a clothes brush, a stack of handkerchiefs and a box containing cufflinks. The second drawer contained a few sets of keys, two pairs of sunglasses and a roll of bandages. One wall was completely covered by a mirrored sliding door. I pulled it aside and found an assortment of men's clothing. So, he *had* got rid of Crystal's clothes. Several pairs of men's shoes were lined up neatly on the cupboard floor. At the end was an inbuilt chest of drawers. This contained underwear, socks and T-shirts. On the shelf at the top were some caps, a tennis racket and a camera.

I was starting to feel disappointed and moved to the second bedroom. This room was smaller than the first and completely bare. The small mirrored cupboard contained nothing but an umbrella and an old television set. The third bedroom could not be seen from the street so I turned on the light and flicked off my torch. There was no wardrobe here—just a bed, a desk and a filing cabinet. The contents of the cabinet showed that Rick Bradshaw was an orderly man.

The files were all in alphabetical order and involved the normal running of a household. I spent time looking through these. I then searched the desk which had three drawers. There was more disappointment here. In the top drawer, were pens, pencils, paper clips, envelopes, and a box of rubber bands. The next drawer was equally disappointing: a passport that looked in order, some bank books which revealed that Rick Bradshaw was far from rich, and a folder with current accounts. The third drawer held a stack of A4 paper. I was about to close it when my eye caught something at the back. There were three Kodak envelopes. Two were quite bulging. In a sprawling hand, written on the first was: *The Top End and Ularu.* I flicked through them. There was Rick on a camel and lots of photos of Ularu, Darwin and Kakadu. The next bulging folder had the same scrawling writing: *Thailand.* Here was Rick on an elephant. The rest of the photos were typical tourist photos. The third smaller envelope had an inscription on the front: *Lunch at The Onion Soup.* This was in different handwriting. I opened it and my heart lurched. There was a photo of Crystal. She was standing with a woman perhaps in her early forties. They had their arms around each other. There were two other photos, both of Crystal and the same woman. I took out one and put it in my pocket. As I did so, I heard the garage door opening. I turned off the light and dashed to the stairs.

Before I got to the bottom, the door to the house opened. I ran across the living room to the sliding door. Thank Christ I had left it open. But a shout from behind told me I had been seen.

'Stop!'

I ran fast up the driveway and into the street, glad that I had parked my car around the corner. If Bradshaw had spotted it, he would have known the identity of his intruder. I turned the corner, hopped in my car, and took off. I didn't turn on my lights until I was around the next corner.

Back home, I studied the photo. Why hadn't Bradshaw showed it to the police? Maybe he had reasons for hiding it.

The next day I phoned Stephanie Darrieux. 'I've got something to show you. It might help your investigation.'

Two hours later I was in Stephanie's office. I showed her the photo. She looked at it briefly and then focused on me with those incredible eyes.

'Where did you get this?' she asked.

'Let's say, I found it.' Darrieux looked back at the photo.

'Who is the woman?' she asked, eyeing me coolly.

'I don't know. But the photo was taken in December 2018. That was the month before Crystal disappeared. I think we should locate that woman.'

'We?' Darrieux asked severely.

'Sorry, you.'

'Does Rick Bradshaw know her?' she asked.

I was afraid this might be Stephanie's first question. If she showed Rick Bradshaw the photo and told him how she came by it, I would be in big trouble. I decided to avoid that tricky situation by lying.

'No, I showed it to Bradshaw. He's got no idea who she is.'

'I'll get our little helpers in the media to run it.' Stephanie stood and walked to the door.

'Are you staying with your aunt for Christmas?' I asked.

'Yes, I'm going up Christmas Day.'

*

On Christmas Eve I drove over to Jaz and Steve's. I wasn't surprised to see Ben's BMW parked in the drive.    On the front path was a rolled-up newspaper. It looked like the local rag. I picked it up and rang the bell.  Jaz greeted me with a kiss and I handed her a bottle of champagne.

Steve, Ben and Danni were out on the back deck. It was just like old times except that Shelly wasn't here. Steve handed me a beer.   I threw the newspaper down on the table and it rolled open.  Darrieux hadn't wasted any time.  There on the front page was the photo of the mystery woman. Crystal's photo had been cut off.  The double-sized caption '*Do You Know This Woman?*' stood out.

Jaz grabbed the paper and frowned.  '*I* know this woman.'

'Who is it?' I asked trying to hide my enthusiasm.

'Let me think.   I've seen her, but I can't remember.'

'She was with Crystal,' I said.

'Of course, that's it.  She came into the office to see Crystal.' Jaz's eyes opened wide as memory flooded her brain. 'That's Crystal's mother,' she whispered.

The news sent a spark of adrenalin through me. If that was Crystal's mother, it must be her birth mother. The adoptive mother had died before that photo was taken.   Why hadn't she come forward when Crystal disappeared? I wondered.

'Did Crystal introduce you to her mother?' I asked.

'No.'

'How did Crystal react when her mother came to the office?' I asked.

-'Oh, she was always so happy after. They'd go out for lunch in Crystal's break. After, her mood would last for hours, and then she would go back to...being Crystal.'

'What do you mean?'

'Crystal was never really relaxed, always a bit sad, a bit guarded. But after her mother's visits, she was a different person, but like I said, only for a while.' Jaz wrinkled her brow. 'But how did you know that woman was connected with Crystal?'

'Darrieux told me.' I lied. I took out my mobile and tapped in Stephanie's number.

I got the answering service but decided against leaving a message.

As Danni and Ben were moving on to another party, we broke up around nine and I drove on home.

# CHAPTER 7
## *Brett*

On Christmas Day my parents travelled to the other side of Sydney to have lunch with Mum's sister. I pretended I was having Christmas lunch with friends. Spending the day alone didn't bother me. In fact, I'd grown used to it over the past three years.

With the intention of working on my book, I took my laptop onto the front deck. Immediately I was distracted by the magnificent view. The wide stretch of golden sand and sparkling ocean were picture perfect and the waves were just right for body surfing. The temptation was too great. I put my work away and made for the beach.

It was only ten but already the sand was well sprinkled with sun lovers. I wandered down to the water's edge and was about to plunge in when I saw her. She was on a boogie board heading for the shore. She hopped off the board, picked it up, and tucked it under her arm. Her usually sleek dark hair was now a tangle of wet curls.

'Merry Christmas', I said to Stephanie Darrieux.

'Merry Christmas to you too. The water's divine,'

she said as I followed her along the beach.

She dumped her board next to a bag, grabbed a towel, and began vigorously rubbing her wet body.

'I've got something to tell you,' I said. She stopped her rubbing and looked at me inquiringly.

'I know who the woman in the picture is.'

'So do I.'

'You know?'

'A past neighbour of the woman's came forward yesterday.' Stephanie threw her towel on the sand and knelt on it. I sat beside her. 'He saw the photo in the Manly Daily. The woman's name is Gabrielle Chambers. She died on the 27th January 2019.'

'That was just after Crystal disappeared. How did she die?'

'It appears she slipped on the bathroom floor and hit her head.'

'She was Crystal's mother.'

Stephanie's eyes widened. 'Her mother?'

'I take it there was a police report?' I asked.

'Oh yes—and I've read through it. There were no signs of foul play. The unit was searched and it was established that she worked in a nearby factory. She had few friends and, it appears, no enemies. There was nothing there to connect her with Crystal. How do you know Gabrielle Chambers was Crystal's mother?'

'According to Jaz, she had been coming into the office to see Crystal.'

'Why didn't Jaz mention this before?' Stephanie eased herself into a sitting position.

I shook my head. 'Maybe she forgot.'

'Did Jaz say how things were between them?'

'Crystal told Jaz that her mother had recently come back into her life and that she was very happy. Apparently, the mother's visits always cheered Crystal.'

'She waited for the adoptive parents to die before contacting Crystal,' murmured Stephanie.

'That could mean that she had been keeping track of Crystal. If that's the case, why wasn't there anything about Crystal in her unit?'

'Good question.' Stephanie stretched out on the towel.

'Crystal was a champion swimmer. There were magazine articles about her. A loving mother would have kept those, you would think,' I said.

There was a short silence during which time I noticed that Stephanie Darrieux had a great pair of legs. She caught me looking.

'It seems an odd coincidence that Crystal disappears one day and her mother dies the next,' said Stephanie.

'What about Crystal's time in detention? Have you looked into that?' I asked.

Stephanie cast me a sidelong glance. 'I've made an appointment with the liaison officers at both detention centres.' She pulled a sheer top out of her bag and slipped it over her head.

'What happened between you and Crystal on the island?' she asked.

'I don't understand why this is so important to everyone. How can it possibly help the investigation?'

'If you two got into an intimate situation, then I'll

bet something was said that might throw some light on this frustrating case.'

'I'll make a deal. If you have dinner with me tonight at Jericho's, I'll tell all.'

Stephanie smiled. 'I could never refuse a dinner at Jericho's.'

*

I picked her up at seven. She was ready but didn't invite me in. She was wearing a soft, floating dress of emerald green. Her beach curls had now been transformed back into a sleek shiny bob and she looked gorgeous.

As we parked, she spoke. 'How on earth did you get a last-minute booking at this restaurant on Christmas night?'

I touched the side of my nose. 'I know people in high places,' I quipped.

The truth was that the head waiter, Tony, was a golfing buddy and he pulled strings to get the table.

It was still daylight as we took our seats. The view over the wide expanse of the beach was superb. I ordered the wine and then she searched my face with those mysterious green eyes. 'I'm waiting,' she said.

'You want to know what we talked about? Well, Crystal told me she was with Bradshaw because he made her feel secure. She also said that she was no longer insecure.'

'I think her security probably improved when her mother turned up,' said Stephanie.

'Yes.'

'Go on,' she prompted.

'She told me she had been abandoned as a baby.' I paused, trying to remember what had been said between us. Stephanie watched me patiently as I prodded my mind.   Fragments were piecing together. 'She asked me about my relationship with Shelly, how I met her, how long I'd been with her.'   I closed my eyes trying to bring it all back.  But a blanket of grey filled my memories. 'I don't remember anything else.'

'What about the bracelet?  You were certain she wasn't wearing one.'

'There was no bracelet on her left hand.'  Once again, I saw Crystal's hand in mine.  I saw the long-tapered fingers and the small bare wrist.  'I held her hand.  I remember clearly.  There was no bracelet,' I said.

'But the other hand?'

'I don't know about the other hand.'

'Danni Melville seemed certain that the bracelet found on the body was Crystal's bracelet.'

I shook my head.  'Danni has a memory like a sieve.  I recall once she couldn't remember her own banking password.  I wouldn't put too much store on what Danni remembers.'

'I have a photo of the bracelet.'   Stephanie reached into her purse and pulled out a small pile of photos.  She handed me one.  It featured a bracelet with green stones set in silver.

'Don't remember it.'  I handed it back.  As I did, I caught a glimpse of one of the other photos.  It looked like Crystal in school uniform.

'What are they?'

Stephanie handed me two photos. 'That's Crystal, just before she was sent to detention. This is the other girl, Rachael Livingstone.' Stephanie handed me a second photo.

They were clearer than the grainy ones Sister Monica had shown me.

'She was very pretty,' I said handing back Crystal's photo. I continued studying Rachael Livingstone. There was something about her that unsettled me. Although she was wearing heavy dark-rimmed glasses, I was drawn to her eyes. Stephanie noticed my studied look.

'Do you know her?' she asked.

'No, I don't think so.' Tony came along to take our order. Neither of us had looked at the menu. 'Working hard, mate?' I asked him.

'Lunch was a nightmare. They were wedged in like sardines. This is heaven by comparison. Now, what can I get you? I can highly recommend the salmon. You don't want to be like the rest of the plebs. I've served so much stuffed turkey and plum pudding today that if I look at another piece of poultry, I think I'll start crowing,' he said in his best 'camp' voice. Although Tony was a straight guy, he loved putting on an act for the customers. He filled our glasses, took our orders and minced off.

Stephanie smiled. There was a comfortable silence between us as we watched the colours of dusk slowly invade the sky while the setting sun threw sheets of gold and pink across the ocean.

Stephanie took a sip of her wine. 'This drug thing

bothers me. Obviously one of the girls was innocent. I hope to learn more when I talk to the people at the detention centres, and I'll be having another talk with Sister Monica.'

'I'm inclined to think the cruiser I saw is connected somehow.'

Stephanie didn't comment.

'What inquiries were made about the cruiser?' I asked.

'The marina was checked. No cruisers of that size had been hired out that weekend.'

'It was a big boat, more likely to have been owned privately.'

'We also checked the marina for privately-owned cruisers. None of the big boys went out that weekend.' she said flatly.

'What about the other marinas?'

'Brett, there was nothing concrete to connect that cruiser with Crystal's disappearance. Don't forget, at the time, it was not a homicide investigation. The time and effort to search every marina's records was just not on.'

'And now?'

'And now it's just too late. No marina in the country would have records of which boats went out on a particular day three years ago.'

'I get the feeling that Crystal's disappearance wasn't taken too seriously by the police.'

'Crystal Morgan had a record.'

'Did that make her life less important?'

Stephanie had no answer to my question.

Just then Tony arrived. He flicked out our serviettes, placed them on our laps with a flourish, and served the entrée. 'Enjoy,' he smiled.

I took a mouthful. 'Not bad.'

Stephanie tried hers. 'Delicious.' We ate in silence for a while.

The wine had relaxed me enough to ask. 'Is there a Mr Darrieux?' Stephanie raised the serviette to her lips before speaking. 'No. I've managed to steer clear of that kind of commitment. And you, no Mrs Carlton?'

'No Mrs Carlton. I took a sip of wine and asked. 'What made you join the police force?'

Stephanie took some time before answering. I noticed a shadow cross her face. Finally, she spoke. 'I had always been interested in law and justice and I was in my final year of Law when my brother was killed. He was murdered. I adored my brother and I was utterly traumatised. The police seemed to be getting nowhere. I uncovered stuff they had missed. As a result, an arrest was made and people were convicted. It was only after that I could come to terms with my grief. I also decided that I was interested in law at the grassroots level, not standing in front of a judge and jury in a courtroom. So, I finished my degree and joined the force.'

'And you never practiced law?'

'I practise law every day.'

Tony came along and cleared away our plates. 'The mushrooms were delicious,' said Stephanie.

'The mushies never fail to please,' grinned Tony.

The rest of the night passed pleasantly and we both avoided talking further about Crystal. At her front door, I kissed Stephanie lightly.

'I can't ask you in. My aunt, you know,' she whispered.

'I know,' I nodded.

# CHAPTER 8
## *Stephanie*

When Brett left, Stephanie felt warm and happy. She knew from the first, she was attracted to this good-looking, intelligent man. But she also knew that he was deeply involved in the Crystal Morgan case and, in fact, could actually be considered a suspect.

It was now seven years since Stephanie had joined the police force and she had never regretted it for a moment. Inspector Manning's corruption had been a pivotal point in her decision and she knew the higher she rose in the ranks, the better able she would be to put a stop to that sort of activity. Her dedication and intelligence had not been missed and her recent ranking of sergeant was an amazing achievement for such a comparatively short period of employment.

Stephanie never dated Brendan Lloyd again and, in order to avoid him, had applied for a position in another district. Brendan hadn't given up easily. He had called to the house numerous times, and his phone calls were on a daily basis for nearly six months. Finally, he accepted the inevitable—Stephanie just wasn't interested in anything or anyone other than her job.

She was often frustrated by the lack of drive and intelligence in some of the staff that was allocated to her. Take Phillip Lockwood, for instance. The man was totally undedicated. All he ever thought about was meeting his mates at the pub after work and watching the footy on the weekend. Now if she had someone like Brett working alongside her, life would be a lot easier. It was clear that Brett had an intelligent way of looking at things. His suspicions of Bradshaw and his curiosity about the mysterious cruiser were both valid. And he was definitely right about one thing—the inquiries at the time of Crystal's disappearance were not thorough enough.

The next morning, she was tempted to go to the beach again. She felt certain Brett would be there. She knew he liked her but she also knew that she must keep him at arm's length at least until this case was finished. Then, maybe, just maybe, she would be looking for more of his company.

# CHAPTER 9
## *Brett*

I checked out the beach the next two days but Stephanie didn't appear. I couldn't stop thinking about the cruiser. It had to be connected with Crystal. The cops had looked at the local marina but there were other marinas in and around Sydney they hadn't bothered about. I decided to make my own inquiries and start with the biggest— D'Albora at Rushcutters Bay on Sydney Harbour. Because of its size and layout, this marina attracted the bigger boats and would be the most likely anchorage place for the mystery cruiser.

I drove out there three days after Christmas. The weather was still brilliant and the temperature had soared to thirty-four degrees. The marina was enormous. Dozens of concrete jetties jutted into the bay. It took over an hour for me to inspect the moored boats. I was looking for ones that resembled the mystery cruiser and was astounded that there were so many of them. I made a note of each one. At the end of the hour, I had fifty-nine boats on my list.

The office was located near the entrance to the marina and I wandered in. Seated at a small, untidy desk was a grizzly-looking man who had obviously spent too much time in the sun. A half-smoked cigarette balanced precariously on his lower lip.

'How can I help you?' he asked without taking his eyes off the papers in front of him.

'I'm looking to buy a decent-sized cruiser. I've looked at the boats moored here and taken note of those that fit my needs,' I said handing him my notebook. He grinned as he looked at my list. 'You could have saved yourself a lot of time if you'd come straight to me. Most of these boats aren't for sale. He took a ledger out of a nearby filing cabinet and made some ticks on my notebook. He handed it back to me. Only four boats had a tick. 'Can I get in touch with the owners?' I asked. He motioned with his hand for me to return the notebook. He consulted his ledger again and wrote in names and telephone numbers. I checked through the names. Nothing rang a bell.

'I'll bet there must be others who would sell if the price is right,' I said, cagily.

'Maybe, but they haven't told me.'

'Could I have a list of all the owners of those other boats?'

He shook his head. 'I don't think I can do that. Privacy, you know.'

'I would have thought that with the way things are today, a lot of these blokes would want to sell.'

'Sorry, mate, no can do.'

'Could I talk with the manager?' I asked.

He scowled at me. 'I am the manager.' He picked up a card and thrust it at me.

'Well, I guess you're the boss.'

Outside, I read the card. The guy's name was Martin Button. I needed to get hold of that ledger but the security system would be as tight as Fort Knox. Breaking in after-hours was not an option. I watched the office. The glass windows gave me a clear view of Martin. Most of the time he was talking on the phone.

Soon after midday, a woman from the nearby café called in with his lunch. He pulled a pie out of one of the bags and started eating. He read a newspaper as he ate. He demolished a lot of food and it was twenty minutes before he finished eating. Then he got up, left the office, and disappeared around the corner. This was my chance. I dashed into the office, made for the filing cabinet, and found the ledger. At a nearby newsagent, I copied all the pages listing the cruisers and their owners.

When I returned to the marina, Martin was back at his desk. I stood behind a brick wall running parallel to his office. There were some gaps in the wall which allowed me to see without being seen. I started going through the ledger, not really knowing what I expected to find. There were so many luxury vessels—so many rich people! Luckily the boats were listed in size, rather than owners' names and I focused on the list of larger boats. And then a name leaped out at me—Lance Gibson! He owned a sixty-five-foot cruiser named Golden Girl and it had berthed at the marina for five years.

I found Golden Girl at the end of jetty 24. She sat shimmering in the sun. It certainly could have been the mystery cruiser. I returned to my post behind the wall. It was now three o'clock. From around the corner, the same woman from the café arrived, this time with a cappuccino and a cake. Martin drank the coffee, ate the cake, and then went off again. By now I suspected he was using the loo. I dashed in and threw the ledger into the drawer.

I drove to Gibson's house in Church Point and parked across the road. A place like this would be littered with security systems. I needed to get in and see if 'Mr Big' had anything to hide. A break-in here wouldn't be the pushover I had experienced at Rick Bradshaw's house. Then it came to me— just go to the front door and knock.

I decided to wait until Gibson was out and make it look like a call on Shelly for old-time's sake. At the same time, I would set a trap. My experience in electronics would make it easy for me to set up a few bugging devices.

I needed help so I confided in Dad. He already knew most of what had happened three years ago and I was relieved when he agreed to help me. Together we worked out a strategy. If Gibson answered, dad would hang up. Luckily Shelly answered and our well-rehearsed plan went into action.

'Is Lance there?' Dad's voice was steady.

I listened in on the extension and heard Shelly say, 'No he's not. Who is this?'

'It's Martin from the marina. I need to talk with Lance about Golden Girl.'

'What about Golden Girl?' asked Shelly.

'One of the bigger cruisers is shooting through and I can offer Lance a better berth. I think he'd be interested.   When will he be back?'

'Not till Thursday.  You can call him then.'

'Thanks, I'll do that.'  Dad winked at me as he dropped his phone into his pocket.  I felt he was enjoying the cloak-and-dagger game. I now knew that Gibson was away for the next three days and decided this was the time to make my move.

The next day I drove to the house in Church Point. A gate at the far end of the property wasn't locked and I entered.  Tropical plants and trees were abundant, and colourful flower beds lined each side of the brick driveway.  The heavy intoxicating scent of a port-wine magnolia filled the air.  Reaching the front porch, I pressed the buzzer.

'Who is it?' I heard Shelly's voice.

'It's Brett.  I was just driving past.' I was trying to keep my voice casual.

A few moments passed and then the door opened.  Shelly was dressed in a bikini with a sheer, loose shirt on top.   She was nursing a half-filled wine glass.

'This is a surprise,' she said ushering me into a huge dimly-lit room.   I followed her to an oversized curved bar.

'Like a drink?'

'A beer would be fine,' I said.  She took a can from the fridge and handed it to me.  We walked out through the double glass doors and onto a sprawling tiled deck. An enormous pool curved its way around the deck.

Shelly sat on a reclining chair and patted the one next to her. I took the cue and sat.  She took a slow slip of her wine and eyed me over the brim of her glass.

'What brings you to my humble abode?' she asked sardonically.

'Hardly humble. What does he do, your husband?'

'He's an importer.'

'Where is he now?' I said pulling the tab on my beer.

'What's it to you?'

'Just making conversation,' I said taking a swig of beer.

'Lance is often called away on business.' She threw me a look that said, 'Don't ask questions.'

'Well, you've got what you always wanted, Shell.'

'There's always a price.' There was a short silence. Then she said, 'And what have you been up to?'

'I'm still writing. My latest tech book is published and it's out to the universities for first semester.'

'I meant your love life.' She cast me a humourless smirk.

'Nothing happening there.'

'I find that hard to believe.'

'Can I get you a refill?' I nodded to her near-empty glass. She handed it to me.

'Get yourself another beer,' she said with a flirty grin. I responded with a wink. I wandered back into the house. Now was my chance. The bar would be a good place for one of my devices, but there didn't seem to be a suitable spot to plant it. I turned my attention back to the big room. A dining table surrounded by chairs occupied an adjoining alcove. This would be a safer bet. I fixed the device beneath the table top as close to the centre as possible and stuck another one under the phone table. I then filled her glass and took out another beer but didn't pull the tab. I needed to place my third device and reasoned that their bedroom would be the ideal place. But how to get there? Outside, I found Shelly climbing out of the pool. I handed her the wine.

'Nice house. Like to give me a 'Cook's' tour?'

'If you want.' She patted her wet body with a towel and tied it around her waist. I followed her back into the house. She walked to the main window area and pressed a button. The heavy brown curtains pulled aside. Immediately the room was flooded with light. Thick oriental rugs covered gleaming timber floorboards. Two brown leather sofas and four single matching chairs faced a huge wall-mounted television set. Another wall was set up as a library with hundreds of books on display. Strategically placed coffee tables matched the heavy oak dining table. The surrounding eight chairs were upholstered in brown patterned fabric matching the curtains.

'Impressive,' I said.

'I hate it. It's Lance's taste, not mine.' She opened a door that led into the long narrow kitchen. Black granite bench tops contrasted with the white polyurethane cupboards. The overall feeling was clinical and neutral. A short hallway led to the study. The furnishings duplicated those in the main living room. The downstairs bathroom featured beige tiles and white basins.

'Boring, isn't it?' she said as she sailed up the stairs. The first five bedrooms carried the brown masculine theme, but when she opened the door to the main bedroom, I was dazzled by the contrast.

'I told Lance if he wanted to sleep with me, the boring crap had to go.'

The king bed was covered with a lime and purple silk bedspread which matched the curtains. The furniture was white and the carpet was cream.

'This is more like you, Shell.'

She walked toward me and took the unopened can of beer from me. She put it on the bedside table and carefully placed her glass next to it. She put her hands on my shoulders. 'You know, I do have everything I ever wanted, except for one thing. I miss the good times we had together. I miss you.'

'*You* left *me*.' I said as I took her shoulders and created a tiny distance between us.

'You betrayed me,' she whispered.

'I don't want to talk about that,' I said.

'Lance is away till Thursday.' She kissed me. My mind was working overtime. I needed to plant the device and this could be the way to go. I kissed her back and pulled her onto the bed. I made a face. 'You smell of chlorine.' I tried to sound casual. But I knew Shelly. She would take the hint. 'I'll wash it off.' She walked to the en suite. I heard the shower turn on. This was my chance. There was enough space between the wall and the bed-head for my hand and I managed to fix the device on the bed-head midway down from the top. I heard the shower go off. I left the room and skipped down the stairs.

I was near the front door when I heard her scream. 'Brett! Where are you going?' She stood at the top of the stairs, naked.

'I've changed my mind.'

'You forgot your beer!' she yelled. I got to the front door. My hand was on the knob when the unopened can of beer crashed into the door. It missed my head by a fraction.

Back in my car, I afforded myself a chuckle. I had planted the devices and got one back on Shelly at the same time. I decided to wait until Gibson returned on Thursday before bothering to listen in on the bugs.

Back home, I phoned Stephanie. 'Hi, it's Brett. Just wanted to let you know that Lance Gibson owns a boat that looks like the one I saw on the river.' There was a brief silence.

'That's interesting. Where is it berthed?'

'At D'Albora Marina, Rushcutters Bay.'

'What's it called?'

'Golden Girl.'

'How did you find out?'

'Shelly Gibson mentioned it.' I lied without any guilt. I had no intention of telling Stephanie how I came by the information or of the bugs I'd just planted.

'I'll check it out,' she said.

'Have you been to the detention centres?' I asked.

'Yes.'

'And?'

'Nothing much came from that,' she said evasively.

'Have you been to see Sister Monica again?' I

asked.

'I'm going tomorrow.'

'Good luck.'

I then phoned the convent. 'Good afternoon. This is Brett Carlton. Detective Darrieux and I have an appointment with Sister Monica tomorrow. I need to confirm the time.'

'I'll look it up for you,' said the receptionist. 'It's three-thirty, Detective Carlton.'

'Thank you.' I suddenly felt emotionally drained. A gym workout was what I needed to get me back on track.

By six, I'd exhausted myself at the gym, but I still couldn't come down. I was jumpy and agitated. I had dinner with my parents and fell into bed around ten. The night was hot and humid and sleep wouldn't come. After two hours of tossing and turning, I got up and wandered out to the deck. The air was heavy and salty and the sea was roaring. I was surprised to see my mother sitting there.

'What are you doing up?' I sat beside her.

'Couldn't sleep,' she said wearily.

'Nor could I,' I murmured.

'Are you okay?' she asked.

'I'm a bit wound up. And you?'

'I'm worried about you.'

'Why?'

'You're getting obsessed with this Crystal business. You know what happened last time.'

'I'm okay.'

'Let the police do their job.'

'They're missing important points.'

'Why do you care?  The girl is gone.  You're still here.'

'I feel responsible.'

'Why?'  Her expression was grave.

'I made love to her that last day.  I can't help but think it was because of that she disappeared.'

'Do you think someone killed her through jealousy?'

'I'm not convinced she's dead.'

'Brett, you had a nervous breakdown three years ago.  You were severely depressed.  You can't go down that path again.'

'I won't.  But I need to know what happened.'

Mum reached over and put her arm on my shoulder.  'Just be careful, son.'

# CHAPTER 10
## *Brett*

The next day I drove to the convent but wasn't sure how I should handle Stephanie. I knew she wouldn't be happy to see me there and might try to keep me out. I arrived ten minutes early.

'Brett Carlton to see Sister Monica,' I said to the receptionist.

'Hello, Detective. You're a little early. Detective Darrieux hasn't arrived as yet.'

'She could be running a bit late. Would it be okay if I saw Sister now?"

'I'll see if she's available.'

Five minutes later I was sitting opposite Sister Monica.

'Is Detective Darrieux still coming?' Monica placed her hands together and surveyed me with gentle eyes.

'I believe so. She should be here any minute.' As I spoke, there was a knock on the door and Stephanie walked in. Her eyes blazed when she saw me.

'Here she is.' I said jovially.

'What are you doing here?' she hissed at me.

Monica looked alarmed. 'What's the problem?' she asked.

'I'm sorry Sister, there's been a misunderstanding. I'm not a Detective. I'm just assisting Detective Darrieux with her investigation.' I cast Stephanie a side-long glance. Her eyes were still blazing as she fought her emotions.

'Oh, I see. Well, I think I've told you all I know.' Stephanie was doing her best to ignore me and her eyes remained focused on Sister Monica.

'You've been very helpful. But since talking to you last, we've learned something about Crystal. We understand that she was a champion swimmer.'

'That's correct. She was a State junior champion.'

'I suppose that would have given her some hero status?'

'Quite the reverse, it seemed to create a wider gap.'

'How come?'

'Crystal was very pretty, beautiful in fact. Some of the girls were already jealous of her. When she did so well at swimming, it apparently increased her unpopularity.'

'Were you aware of this?'

'No, none of us were. It came out later, not long before the drug incident. Crystal came to my office, very distressed. She said that Rachael Livingstone had been causing trouble and that she was running a bullying campaign against her. This was quite concerning as Rachel was in a higher class and was nearly two years older.

I offered to look into it but she said it wouldn't do any good. She just wanted to leave the school.' Sister Monica looked down at her hands while she gathered her thoughts. 'I said she only had a year to go and should stick it out. I reminded her that the New South Wales junior swimming championships were not far off and she should be training. She then told me she hated swimming and was only doing it because her parents were pushing her. She said that once she was free to make her own decisions, she would never swim again.'

I looked at Stephanie. I could see that she was getting the same message as me. Crystal told everyone she couldn't swim simply because she didn't *want* to swim. There was probably nothing furtive about her story.

'What happened then?' asked Stephanie.

Monica's voice tightened. 'I had a word with Crystal's mother. She was adamant that Crystal would stay at school and continue training for the championships. She said Crystal would just have to toughen up and ignore the bullying. Crystal continued training and won the title a month or so later.'

'Do you think Crystal had a good relationship with her parents?' I asked. Stephanie cast me an angry look. She obviously objected to my interference.

Monica replied. 'No. I don't think Crystal had a good relationship with either of her parents. This became apparent when Crystal was arrested. They seemed to disassociate themselves from her.'

'What exactly happened?' asked Stephanie.

'Nothing, that's just it—they did nothing. Crystal

had no legal representation, and I believe that was one of the reasons she was convicted.'

'So, you don't believe she was guilty?' I asked.

'I don't pretend to be an expert on people's behaviour and I could be completely wrong, but I believed Crystal was innocent.'

'And Rachael Livingstone?' asked Stephanie.

'I don't know.' Sister Monica looked steadily at us, and I felt that she had said all that she wanted to say.

'Thank you, Sister, you've been very helpful. Hopefully, we won't be bothering you again.' Stephanie stood.

We walked together through the hall and out into the garden. Then Stephanie turned on me. 'How dare you interfere in my investigation! You lied your way into that nun's office and tried to take over my interview. Just don't do it again!' She walked briskly as she spoke.

'I'm in this whether you like it or not,' I said.

She stopped and turned to face me. 'You might be part of this investigation but you're not an investigator. And don't forget, you are still a suspect!' She strode through the gate and headed for her car.

I waited until she was out of sight and headed back to the convent. I spoke to the receptionist who still thought I was a detective. 'Sorry to worry you again. But I forgot to ask Sister Monica the names of the two detention centres where Crystal and Rachael were sent. Do you have them there?' I waved a casual hand to the stack of files on her desk.

'I should have it. I got the file out when I knew you were coming. It's here somewhere.' She searched

through the stack. 'Ah, here it is,' she said smiling.
She leafed through the pages. The caption on the front
of the manila folder read 'Morgan and Livingstone'.

'Here we are. Rachael was sent to Dalway on the
Central Coast and Crystal went to Morrison at Windsor.

The next day I headed to Windsor and the
detention centre. It was a long drive and I got there
around eleven. An eight-foot brick wall encompassed
the entire area which was the size of a football field.
Entry was through a pair of heavy timber gates.
Immediately inside the grounds, a barricade prevented
further progress. A guard asked about my business and
presented me with a form to fill in. I also had to show
identification before being allowed through the barricade.

I walked along a narrow concrete path to the big
sprawling building. Groups of people wandered around
the yard. It was hard to tell if they were staff or inmates.
A vain attempt had been made to create gardens, but
straggling weeds seemed to be faring better than the sad
clumps of dusty flowers struggling to survive.

Tall timber doors opened into a huge entry hall.
Cheap linoleum on the floor emitted a strong waxy smell.
At the reception desk, a woman was working at a
computer. She was aware of my presence but continued
to type and ignore me. I stood patiently. After a few
minutes, I spoke. 'Excuse me. I'm trying to get details
about a former inmate.' The woman squinted at me over
her glasses. 'You from the police?' she asked in a
croaky voice.

'No,' I said.

She frowned at me. 'Name, please.'

'Brett Carlton.'

'Where are you from?'

'I'm a private citizen.'

'You will have to speak with the liaison officer. I'll see if he's around.' She hit the intercom and I noticed her fingers were heavily stained with nicotine. I could clearly hear the other end when a male voice answered. 'Yes?'

The woman spoke. 'A Mr Carlton is here. Can you see him?'

'Does he have an appointment?'

'No, he doesn't.' There was a brief silence.

Then the man spoke again. 'What's it about?'

'Who is this former inmate?' she asked me.

'Her name is Crystal Morgan. She disappeared three years ago, believed murdered. She is, *was* a friend of mine.'

'It's about Crystal Morgan,' said the woman into the intercom.

'Send him up. I can give him ten.'

'Up the stairs, first door on your left,' she croaked.

I walked up the bare concrete stairs. The office door was open.

'Come in,' called a gruff voice. 'Close the door behind you,' barked the man. I did as I was told. 'Sit down,' he ordered.

I was starting to feel like a subordinate soldier.

'Graham Bushell.' He held out a fat hand.

'Brett Carlton,' I said shuffling into the seat.

Bushell's eyes squinted at me from the folds of his bulldog face. 'What do you want to know?' he asked.

'I'm after some information about Crystal Morgan.'

'Are you with the police?'

'No.'

'Well, they were in here earlier this week about the same person.  What's your connection?'

'She was my girlfriend.'

'And?'

'I'd like to know just what sort of an inmate she was.  Did she get into trouble?  Did she have friends?'

Bushell put his head to one side and screwed up his narrow eyes.

I went on.  'You see, Crystal never told me she had been in detention.  I only found out after...after she went missing.'

'Yes, on the boat.  We know about that.'

'The police think she's dead.  I think she could still be alive.  That's why I'm looking into her past.'

'They found a body, didn't they?'

'Yes. but it hasn't been identified.  I would be very grateful if you could help me.  It's been a very difficult time for me.'  I bowed my head and put my hand to my eyes.   I knew I was laying it on a bit thick, but strangely, I didn't feel deceptive.  I was genuinely feeling deeply emotional.

'Well, I can only tell you what I told the police. Crystal Morgan was an ideal inmate.  She kept her nose clean and behaved well.  She was a bit of a loner, didn't seem to have any friends.  She completed her Higher School Certificate and started a correspondence course in graphic design. She got an early release for good behaviour.'

'Is that all you can tell me?'

Bushell frowned before speaking. 'There was an incident. Actually, there were two incidents. Crystal was heard talking to...herself. She claimed she had been talking to a visitor. But no one was there. Then it happened again. This time, I was concerned and called in a psychiatrist. She had a few sessions with him.'

'And?' I asked.

'Nothing. The psychiatrist found no evidence of psychosis. He prescribed a mild sedative and said she was merely suffering from stress.'

'And then?'

'She was released soon after.'

'Where did she go?'

'She went back to her parent's place. We kept an eye on her for a while. One of our officers became her case manager and kept us informed. She apparently settled back into the community, and got a job.'

Bushell stood, walked to the door, and held it open. I was surprised when he put his hand on my shoulder as I passed him. 'Good luck,' he said.

I looked at my watch. It was just after midday. I decided to tackle Rachael Livingstone's past and headed up the coast. It was mid-afternoon before I reached Dalway Detention Centre. This place was smaller than Morrison but the layout was similar.

Again, I was sent to the Liaison Officer. 'Come in,' came the reply to my knock on the half-opened door.

A sixty-something woman sat at a big, old-fashioned desk. Her jet-black hair was pulled back exaggerating her long pointed nose. She introduced herself as Alison McCutcheon. With a stiff smile, she invited me to take a seat. I explained why I was there. She looked at me for a long while and I wondered if she would ever speak. Then she said. 'We talked with Detective Darrieux a few days ago. As this is a murder investigation, I don't think it would be proper for me to talk with you at all.'

'I believe Rachael Livingstone framed Crystal Morgan. It's important for me to know more about her. I think Crystal could still be alive.'

'I'm sorry. If you want that information, you will have to talk to the police.'

'At least can you tell me where Rachael Livingstone went after her release?'

'No,' Alison McCutcheon said curtly. She stood and almost hopped to the door. She was wearing a black-and-white striped top and a black skirt. It struck me that she looked incredibly like a magpie. She opened the door and stood holding it. I hurried past, desperate to avoid a peck from that vicious-looking beak.

I wanted to know more about Rachael and I knew Stephanie had the answers. But I also knew she would still be mad at me. I had to give her time to calm down before asking questions.

# CHAPTER 11
## *Brett*

In the meantime, I had Shelly and Gibson to think about. Tomorrow was Thursday and I had some eavesdropping to do. I decided to wait until evening before trying out the devices. I felt agitated all day and spent time catching up with work-related matters on my computer.

I had a snack around six-thirty and then headed out to Church Point. It was almost dark when I reached Gibson's house. I needed to find an area that would allow a clear pathway from transmitter to receptor. I decided the street running parallel to theirs was perfect. I turned on all three receptors. There was nothing coming from the bedroom. The dining room was emitting cluttering sounds like crockery and cutlery being shifted around. Then I heard her voice. I was excited by the clarity.

'You've got to call Marty at the marina,' said Shelly. A scraping sound of metal on plates told me they were eating dinner.

'What's he want?' said Gibson.

'He's got a new berth for Golden Girl.'

'She doesn't need a new berth.  The one I've got is fine.  When did he call?'

'Monday.'

'What else did he say?'

'Just that one of the other cruisers was going and you could have the berth.'

'He's off his tree.  The idiot knows I like my berth. You didn't say we'd take the other one, did you?'

'Course not.'

'Well, it was still there when I got in today.  He'd better not give it away if he wants to live.'

'Where's the stuff?'

'Bunny picked it up.  He's keeping it at his place and then shifting it on the weekend.'

'How much?'

'Ten kilos.'

'How much money, dopey?'

'Enough.'

'I want some plastic surgery.'

'What now?'

'I'm getting wrinkles.'

'I don't see any wrinkles.'

'You need glasses.  Talking of glasses, mine's empty.'

I then heard the scraping of chairs and glasses clinking.  I could hear eating sounds, and in the background, voices and music.  I guessed the television had been turned on, and I didn't pick up any more conversation.

It was two hours before the bedroom transmitter

came to life. I heard noises like doors opening and closing and a toilet flushing. The sounds went on for around twenty minutes. Then silence. An hour later, I heard similar noises. Soon after, I heard a regular snoring sound. I guessed that Shelly had come to bed first followed later by Gibson. They were now both asleep. I felt envious as I badly needed sleep myself. I turned off my receptors and headed home. I felt the exercise had been fruitful. They were up to something. The stuff that weighed ten kilos and was valuable, could only be one thing—drugs.

The next night I parked my car closer to the house. This time I took Mum's car, I decided that switching cars would prevent any unwanted suspicion. I was setting up my receptors when I saw a van pull up outside the house. A huge man stepped up to the intercom on the gate. I grabbed my binoculars. The guy was built like an ox. His massive arms were covered in tattoos and he looked like a heavyweight wrestler. The gates opened and his car disappeared into the grounds. Within minutes I heard Gibson say, 'Like a drink, Bunny?'

'Yeah...I could do with one.' The voice was like gravel. There was a clinking of glasses. So, this was Bunny, the guy Gibson said was shifting the stuff. I heard Bunny's husky voice again. 'Thanks. It's all been sorted and here's your dough.'

There was a silence and then Gibson spoke again. 'Good, here's your cut. Cash as agreed. Count it if you like.'

'No need. I trust ya.' There was a break in the conversation. I heard furniture moving and footsteps.

Then Gibson spoke again. 'Did you check out the marina like I asked?'

'Yeah. Marty reckoned he never phoned to offer a new berth.'

'Was anyone poking around Golden Girl?'

'Not that Marty knew. But he said a bloke came in asking about big cruisers for sale. Marty gave him the names of some guys wanting to sell. The guy asked for a list of all the owners. Marty wouldn't give it.'

'Did Marty get the name of this man?'

'No. He said he was a young guy, tall, good looking, that's all.'

'We'll be late if we don't get moving.' I heard Shelly's voice.

'I'll be off. When's the next run?' asked Bunny.

'I'll call you,' said Gibson. I heard footsteps and then a door opening and closing. More footsteps and then the bedroom receptor came to life just as I saw Bunny's car screech out into the street. I got a good look at his big rough head as he drove past.

Muted bedroom sounds continued for nearly ten minutes. Then I heard Shelly's voice. 'I've lost my diamond earring.'

'For Christ's sake, just get ready.' said Gibson.

'I had them on last night. I took them off in bed. There was one on the floor. The other one has to be here.' I heard muffled dragging noises. 'What's this?' said Shelly. There were a few scraping noises and then Gibson's furious voice.

'Christ, it's a fucking bug behind our bed! How did it get here, Shell?' I heard Gibson's menacing voice.

'How would I know?'

'Who's been in this room?'

'No one, only the cleaner.'

'The same cleaner we've had for five years?'

'Yes. She's okay.'

'I know she's okay. I hired her. Who have you been entertaining, sweetheart?'

'No one.' I heard a slap and Shelly's painful groan.

'I've got recording cameras all over the house. Just save me the effort. Tell me who it was.'

'Brett Carlton called in on Monday.'

'And you had a little play in our bedroom.'

'No. He wanted to see through the house.'

'And you let him wander around, free as a bird?'

'I was with him all the time. He wasn't out of my sight.'

'You'll have to do better than that.'

'I did leave him, only for a minute. I went to the bathroom.'

'Stupid bitch. And where else might he have bugged?'

'Nowhere else.'

I was grateful Shelly had forgotten about me going to the bar.

'Great,' Gibson mumbled sarcastically. 'And he's probably heard everything.'

There were some noises like drawers slamming and then Gibson spoke loudly and deliberately. 'Mr Nosey Carlton will have to pay for this.' A short knock told me the device had been unplugged. I turned the other two receptors back on.

After a minute or two, the receptor under the phone table came to life. 'Bunny? Where are you now?' There was a pause. I couldn't hear the other end. Then Gibson spoke again. 'Good. I've got a job for you. It's worth half a grand. I want it done *now*. Go to 20 Plantation Road, Newport. A certain Brett Carlton needs some roughing up. If you can't find him, there are a couple of oldies who can take his place. Remember— no dead bodies, just a rough up.'

My throat went dry. I knew it wouldn't take Bunny long to get to the house. I called home and was relieved when Mum answered straight away.

'Mum, you and Dad have to get out of the house now. You don't have a minute to waste. You're in danger. Just get in the car and go. No questions. Get out now!' I drove like a demon and arrived at the house in record time. After parking in the driveway, I called Stephanie's number. 'I don't have time to give you details but I've stumbled onto something which has put me and my parents in danger. I'm at the house and about to go in. I don't know what to expect but it's possible that I could be walking into trouble.'

'You're at your parents' house?'

'Yes.'

I jumped out of the car and ran to the front door. It was unlocked. Inside, I hit the light switch. Nothing happened. All the electricity had been disconnected. The curtains were drawn and the blackness was intense. I remembered that Dad kept the torches in the linen cupboard. I grabbed one and played the beam around the room. Everything looked in order. I checked the kitchen and the downstairs bathroom. Then I heard a noise from upstairs. It was like a footstep on a creaking board. I knew I could be walking into a trap but I had to make sure my parents were out of the house. I walked up the stairs and went straight to my bedroom. At first, it seemed I was alone. Then, I was aware of a presence behind me. I was about to turn when my conscious world came to an abrupt end as what seemed like an iron mallet crashed into my head.

# CHAPTER 12
## *Stephanie*

Stephanie drove away from the convent feeling angry and irritated by Brett's interference in her investigation. He had really stepped over the line this time. How dare he barge in on her interview with Sister Monica! But a small voice whispered in her ear: *You did the same thing yourself once.* She allowed the tightness in her jaw to relax as she remembered how she had interfered in her brother's murder investigation and how that had reaped its rewards.

She returned to headquarters and began her search into Lance Gibson's past. She uncovered some startling results. Gibson had been charged with drug smuggling back in 2018. Although he had been acquitted, the coastal police had continued to put him and his boat under surveillance for more than a year. Stephanie decided it was time Lance Gibson and his Golden Girl were put under surveillance again. She put the wheels in motion.

For the next two days, she worked solely on the Crystal Morgan murder. On Friday afternoon, she turned off her computer and stretched her aching legs.

This case was irritating and frustrating and she needed some peace and quiet. She looked forward to a pleasant night in her apartment with maybe some wine, some music, and a good book in bed.

Three years earlier, Stephanie decided that it was time she cut her parents' apron strings. She did this in spite of wails of protest from Estelle who was still grieving for Jordan. She contacted an estate agent and within a few weeks found a lovely inner-city apartment situated on the thirty-eighth floor. Up so high, she felt safe and secure. An added bonus was the wonderful view of Sydney Harbour that thrilled and entertained her every day. She had enjoyed decorating her new home and selecting her furniture. She had used cream and aqua as accessory colours and complimented the furnishings with some marvellous prints and paintings.

Now in the comfort of her apartment, Stephanie looked out onto the sparkling city lights and the iconic Sydney Harbour Bridge which was glowing against the darkening sky. She poured herself a large glass of white wine and put on a compact disc. She fell into a chair and kicked off her shoes. The magical tones of Pavarotti and Ghiaurov singing the duet from the 'Pearl Fishers' filled the room. She closed her eyes and sighed with sheer pleasure as the magical music sent shivers up her spine. Stephanie's love of classical music had been fostered by her father. Henri Darrieux had been an accomplished violinist and he had enrolled both his children in piano lessons. Jordan gave up at an early age but Stephanie persisted and passed all the Conservatorium piano exams.

She was pouring herself a second glass of wine when her mobile phone rang. It was Brett, and he sounded frantic. His message was short but succinct—he and his parents were in danger. Stephanie immediately made the necessary phone calls, pulled on her shoes, and left the apartment. She had alerted police stations at Dee Why and Chatswood. Hopefully, there would be a car or two in the Newport area. As she suspected, traffic was a nightmare.

She didn't quite know what to expect. But she trusted Brett and his judgment. If he said he was in danger, then she had to believe it. It took her forty minutes to get to the house even with her siren blaring. Two police cars were parked outside with their blue lights flashing. Inside the drive, an ambulance stood with its back doors open. As she walked up the path, two ambulance officers emerged from the house carrying a stretcher. Stephanie felt a sense of dread as she approached it. She looked down onto Brett's pale, unconscious face.

'What happened? How is he?'

'He's had a knock on the head. We won't know how bad he is until we get him to hospital,' said one of the officers as they continued on to the ambulance. Stephanie ran alongside them. 'Which hospital?'

North Shore,' he said, sliding Brett into the ambulance. He climbed in after the stretcher and then pulled the door shut. The other man got into the driver's seat and within seconds, the ambulance sped off with its siren blaring.

As Stephanie walked despondently to the front

door, the house phone rang. She entered and found the phone in the living room. 'Hello? This is Stephanie Darrieux.'

A quiet voice answered. 'This is Rosemary Carlton. Is my son Brett there?'

'I'm afraid he's been injured. He's been taken to hospital.'

Stephanie heard a muffled sob on the other end. 'How bad is it?'

'We don't know. I'm sorry.'

'Which hospital?'

'North Shore."

'We'll go straight there,' said Rosemary as she hung up.

A policeman descended the stairs. Stephanie showed him her badge. 'What happened?'

'He was attacked upstairs in one of the bedrooms. The house was in darkness when we arrived. Someone, probably the intruder, turned off the power. There was no sign of anyone when we got here.'

'Thank you. I'd like someone to go over the place and collect fingerprints.'

Stephanie suddenly felt exhausted. She stayed around for a while and then headed back home. She called the hospital on the way and was told that Brett was still being assessed and treated. There was no other news. She decided she would visit him the next day.

# CHAPTER 13
## *Brett*

I awoke feeling as if my head was in a vice. I heard voices. After a while, I managed to open my eyes. At first, all I saw was a sea of green. The green receded and I eventually focused on Stephanie leaning over me. As hazy as I was, I was conscious of her beautiful green eyes and the matching green silk dress she was wearing.

'Hello,' she said softly. I tried to speak but nothing would come. My mother and father were standing on the other side of the bed. Their faces were sad and tearful. They both looked older than when I had last seen them. Have I been unconscious for years? I wondered. And then the blackness came again.

The next day I felt a lot better. I had a fractured skull but luckily no brain damage. Stephanie came again. 'Do you think you're well enough to talk about it?' she asked.

'Yes, I'm fine.'

Stephanie moved toward me and sat on the bedside chair. 'After you called that night, the night you were attacked, I sent a squad to your house. Your attacker had gone. You knew someone was out to get you. Do you know who it was?'

'Yes. It was a guy called Bunny.'

Stephanie gave me a quizzical look. I then told her all about the bugging devices. She listened attentively and then she spoke. 'I hope you've learned a lesson. None of this would have happened if you had left the detecting to us.'

'I felt you weren't interested in Gibson or his cruiser.'

'That's where you're wrong. I looked up past records and apparently, Gibson and Golden Girl were under surveillance four years ago.'

'Why?'

'There was a tip-off that drugs were being dropped in a certain place at a certain time. A police helicopter saw Golden Girl retrieve some cargo from the sea. The boat was apprehended and searched. As suspected, the cargo was drugs, and Gibson was arrested. He claimed he just saw the stuff floating there and picked it up. He said he didn't know what it was. He had a top lawyer and got off. But for the next twelve months, he and his boat were under surveillance.'

'And now?'

'Gibson and Golden Girl are under surveillance again.'

'And?'

'Nothing. Gibson and his kind can usually pick when they're being watched. He and Shelly are spending a lot of time at home. They're behaving like nice, normal folks.' Stephanie got up, walked to the window, and turned to me. 'I think I know who this Bunny is. I'll bring some mug shots around tomorrow.'

The next day Stephanie arrived early. I was arguing with the nurse. 'Look, I'm okay. I want to go home.'

'Dr. Maloney will say when you can go,' she said stiffly as she dropped the chart into the receptacle at the end of the bed.

Stephanie was hovering around the doorway. She walked in and sat on the edge of the bed. 'You must be getting better. Back to your argumentative and obstinate self, I see.'

'There's nothing wrong with me,' I growled.

'Here are the mug shots.' She handed me a couple of photos. There was a full-faced shot and two side profiles. There was no doubt. It was Bunny.

'Yep. That's Bunny. That's the guy who took the order from Gibson.'

'Bruno Vesalik, known in the underworld as Bunny. He has a record for assault, drug dealing, car theft—you name it.'

'What are you going to do?' I asked.

'I've decided to leave him free for the time being and see where he leads us. Unfortunately, your tapes are inadmissible as evidence.'

'That seems ridiculous. Can't you get a warrant to search Gibson's place?'

'We don't have enough on him.' Stephanie fiddled with the gold chain around her neck and eyed me intently. 'There's something I think you deserve to know. I went to the detention centre where Rachael

Livingstone served her time. Apparently, she wasn't a model prisoner and she had some enemies there. I checked them out. One moved to Tasmania and the other was killed in a car accident a few months after release. So, nothing came from that line. But Rachael had one visitor. He came frequently.' Stephanie took a deep breath. 'It was Lance Gibson.'

I whistled. 'This is getting weirder and weirder. Lance Gibson seems to be in the middle of everything.' We both sat silently trying to find the missing link.

'What happened when Rachael left detention?' I asked.

'The Board likes to keep an eye on juveniles after release, help them get back into society. They found a bed-sitter for Rachael in the inner west and set her up with a job in a furniture store. When the Board made its first monthly check, she had gone—left the flat and left the job. She seemed to have disappeared into thin air.'

'Did they catch up with her?'

'No. She was never located.'

'Could she be dead?'

'It's possible. That's one of the reasons I checked on her enemies in detention.'

*

Soon after leaving the hospital, I realised I still had a way to go before getting back to regular life. But I found the energy to check out my bugging receptors. All transmission had been lost. Gibson had found the other two devices.

I had great concern for my parents' safety and felt my presence was endangering them. I was stuck in

Sydney and there seemed no option for me to return yet to Port Stephens. I took them aside. 'I want you to have a holiday up at my place.'

Mum shook her head. 'We are not leaving you.'

'Look, Mum. I've already put you two in danger. It could have been you that got hit on the head.'

'Your mother's right, Brett. You're still recovering. You shouldn't be left alone.' Dad's voice was firm and serious.

'Don't you see? If I hadn't been concerned about you two, I would never have been attacked. I would have run. Instead, I went upstairs, thinking you were in danger.' I felt I was being a bit cruel saying this and I saw the hurt look that came over my mother's face, but I knew it was the only way I could get them to leave. No one spoke. They were mulling over what I had said. 'Besides, I need someone to water my plants and pick up my mail,' I said brightly.

'You think our presence puts you at worse risk?' asked Mum.

'I do.' I rose and put my arm around her shoulders. 'You are the two most important people in my life.' I kissed her cheek.

Two days later I waved my parents off.

# CHAPTER 14
## *Brett*

I took things easy for the next three weeks and then Stephanie arrived. 'This is a nice surprise,' I said as I ushered her into the house.

'I took an early mark. I'm spending the weekend at my aunt's. She's gone away and I offered to look after Champ.'

'Champ?'

'Her beautiful border collie.' Stephanie wandered to the cocktail cabinet, picked up a family photo, and studied it thoughtfully. After a minute, she replaced the photo and eyed me intently. 'How are you feeling?'

'Fine. Anything happening out at Church Point?'

'Nothing. Golden Girl hasn't budged and the Gibsons are still lying low.'

'And Vesalik?'

'Leading his normal life.'

'Which is?'

'He spends most of his time at the local pub playing pool.'

Just then Stephanie's mobile rang. I could see by the expression on her face this was an important call.

She listened to the caller for several minutes before speaking: 'Interesting ... Good. I'll get back to you.' She popped the phone back into her bag. 'That was the officer outside Gibson's house. He said there's been a lot of activity there. Truckloads of flowers, grog and food have been rolling in all day. He managed to talk to a guy in a catering van. Apparently, the Gibsons are throwing a big party tonight. One hundred people have been invited. He even got hold of an invitation...don't ask me how. The party is celebrating the 'Ides of March' and everyone is invited to come masked and in costume.'

'Wow. Do you suppose Gibson might be planning something? With one hundred people all disguised, it would be easy for him to slip through the surveillance.'

'Possibly.'

'Stephanie, this could be your chance to get into the house. With the right outfits, we could crash the party without being recognised.'

Stephanie eyed me coolly. 'You are a slow learner. I thought I made it clear. This is a police investigation and you are not the police...but the idea is good.'

'Stephanie, I know the house...every room.'

'You can draw me a plan.'

'I can't draw.'

'An engineer and you can't draw? Pull the other one,' she said scornfully.

'Marie Antoinette and King Louis,' I said grinning.

'What?'

'That's who we'll be. I know where to get the

costumes. It will be the perfect disguise. There are wigs as well as masks. They'll never know it's us.'

'You can get the costumes but make sure the male one fits Lockwood.'

'Lockwood? You'd take that undernourished runt? He'll stand out like a sore thumb. He'll never carry it off.'

Stephanie's brow creased in thought. She ran her hand through her hair. 'We'll see.' She took out her mobile. 'Tanner? It's Darrieux. Let me know when the guests start arriving tonight.' She dropped the phone into her bag and fixed me with a steady gaze. 'Get the costumes. I'll be back here at seven-thirty.' She headed down the stairs.

'You're a size ten?' I called. She stopped and looked back. 'Yes. How did you know?'

'I'm an expert on women's bodies.' She continued down the stairs without a word. 'God, why did I say that?' I groaned to myself.

I drove to the costume hire place. All the way there I was hoping and praying that the two outfits would be available. Inside the shop, I started sorting through the various costumes. There were witches, ghosts, apes, fairies, nuns, priests, Robin Hoods, pirates, dragons, Draculas, but not the ones I wanted. I turned to the salesgirl. 'You used to have Marie Antoinette and King Louis costumes. Are they out?'

'Yes, a couple came in today. Are you going to the big party at Church Point?' she asked.

'Yes.'

'It's been a real money spinner for us. We've

hired out half the shop.'

'So, I see. I'm really disappointed. Is there anyone else who might have those costumes?'

'Oh, you wouldn't want to go in the same outfit as someone else, would you? Why not try Peter Pan and Wendy?' she said reaching for two costumes.

'I don't care if we're the same as someone else. That's who we want to be.'

'Well, I've got a spare set. We keep at least two of every costume.'

'Why didn't you say so?'

'You didn't give me the chance,' she said sulkily. 'I'll get them for you. 'Can't understand why you'd want to be the same as someone else,' she muttered as she walked off to the adjoining room.

Back home I tried on my costume. It fitted perfectly. The mask covered the top part of my face and the silver wig with a curling tail at the back completely covered my dark hair. But my mouth was visible. Shelly knew my mouth only too well. I decided to make up a moustache. I cut some of my hair and spent the next hour making one.

Stephanie arrived at seven-thirty. I was ecstatic to see that she came without Lockwood and I offered her a drink. 'I'm on duty. And although you are not, I suggest that you abstain too.'

'We'll be offered grog at the party,' I said.

'We can take it but we don't drink it. Now show me the outfits.'

Stephanie took hers into the spare bedroom. I changed into mine complete with wig and moustache, and wandered out to the kitchen. I ignored Stephanie's warning and poured myself a beer. And then Stephanie entered. I was stunned. She looked fabulous. The billowing silk skirt emphasised her tiny waist and the silver wig gave her an ethereal look. She looked authentic and beautiful. I took her hand and, with a bow, kissed it. She did a little curtsy and then wandered to the window and looked out. After a while, she spoke. 'Were you in love with Crystal Morgan?'

'I think I was.'

'You hadn't known her long.' Her voice was oddly accusing. I said nothing.

'How did you feel about Shelly?'

'What do you mean?'

'You were still living with Shelly when you met Crystal.'

'Yes. But that relationship had run its race.'

'How come?'

'We'd been arguing a lot. And she was working shifts two or three nights a week.'

'She was pretty upset about you and Crystal.' Just then, Stephanie's mobile went off. She listened for a few seconds and spoke. 'Thanks, Tanner.' She grabbed her bag. 'Time to go.'

Her car was parked in my driveway. She handed me the keys and I slid into the driver's seat.

'Fifty guests have already arrived. The gates are open and a guy is checking invitations. Our man has an invitation. He'll be waiting in Decklett Street,' Stephanie said.

I remembered this was the street where I'd parked when using the listening devices. It was a small street and the policeman's unmarked car was easy to find.

We parked in front of it, and Tanner came up to the passenger window and handed Stephanie a card. She quickly read it. 'Good work. So, we are Mr and Mrs Conte How did you get this?'

'Let's say I bought it.'

'Thanks, Tanner. Stick around. We might need you,' Stephanie murmured.

Tanner gave a little salute. I drove to the house and lined up behind a few cars at the gates. The gatekeeper had a torch and was checking the invitations. I drew alongside and handed ours over.

'There's parking around the side of the house.' He waved in that direction and handed me back the invitation. 'Have a ball, Mr and Mrs Conte,' he drawled.

'Thanks, I'm sure we will.' I slowly navigated the car around the circular driveway and parked alongside countless other cars.

Stephanie turned to me. 'I think you should let me do the talking if Shelly speaks to us. She knows your voice.'

'True. What are you planning?'

'We'll mix and mingle and then I'll look around for locked rooms. These will be the ones I'll be searching.'

'How can you search them if they're locked?'

Stephanie threw me a sly grin and reached into the pocket of her skirt. She held up a bunch of keys. 'Every policeman's little miracle worker. One of these will do the trick. I can guarantee it.'

We put on our masks and showed our invitation to a man at the front door. He was dressed as a Roman soldier. 'Good evening, Sir and Madam. Welcome to the Ides of March. How should I introduce you?'

'Queen Marie Antoinette and King Louis the Sixteenth,' I said regally.

The man had a microphone and his voice boomed. 'Queen Marie Antoinette and King Louis the Sixteenth.' Stephanie took my arm and we walked into the huge room. People eyed us as we entered. A waiter dressed as a Roman centurion served us champagne. Stephanie frowned as I took a sip.

The atmosphere was amazing. It was as if we had entered another world. All the furniture had been removed and in its place were fake Roman ruins and Roman statues. The walls were covered with scenes of stone pillars, arches and gardens. The glass doors leading out to the pool were wide open. Outside, guests were gathered, and again the theme of ancient Rome was evident. Statues, pillars and Roman art decorated the entire area. Lights had been strung up over the pool giving the water an incandescent glow, and a small fountain had been erected in the centre, sprouting coloured water. The effect was stunning.

We were joined by a woman whose seven-veiled skirt told me she was Salome. She wore a mask but her tall frame and strong arms gave her away. It was Shelly.

'We have another Marie Antoinette and Louis here tonight. Seems a popular choice.' She eyed Stephanie with a furrowed brow. 'You seem familiar but

I'm having trouble placing you. The other Marie Antoinette was easy to pick,' she said.

'Will you be dancing the seven veils tonight, Salome?' asked Stephanie, cleverly diverting the conversation.

'No. And will you lose your head tonight, Marie Antoinette?'

'I hope not.'

'I'll bet before the clock strikes twelve and before all masks are removed, I will have guessed your identity.'

'We'll see,' said Stephanie.

'And your handsome king. What has he to say for himself?'

'He is overcome with your beauty, fair Salome. He cannot speak.'

I was relieved when Napoleon came over and asked Shelly for a dance.

A fake cave had been set up at the far end of the pool. Inside, a six-piece band was beating out very un-Roman music. I noticed there were three Julius Caesars and one of these was Gibson.

A tipsy Joan of Arc staggered over. 'You two are just divine. The other French king and queen failed dismally. You've really flattened them.' She grinned coquettishly at me and glancing at Stephanie said:

'Do you mind if I steal your king for a little dance?' Without waiting for a reply, she grabbed my arm. I looked quickly at Stephanie who nodded with an amused grin.

'I'd be honoured,' I said. I was getting into my part, and the old-fashioned language was coming easily.

I wished I could remember some of my limited French, but only a few phrases came to mind. Joan tripped over my feet as I tried to steer her around the dance floor. I wondered how she would ever survive the rest of the the night. Then I saw Stephanie climbing the stairs. Joan wanted to jive on but I broke away, pleading my desperate need for another drink. I grabbed one from a Roman soldier telling myself I could easily keep a clear head. I blotted out Stephanie's words of warning and took a mouthful. As I did so, I felt a presence. I turned and faced Lance Gibson.

'Great outfit,' he said.

'Great party,' I replied. 'Where did you get all the sets? They're fabulous.'

'I've got my contacts.' He smiled, eyeing me cautiously. 'You know, I reckon I've guessed all the people here tonight. But I can't get you—or your beautiful queen.'

'Is there a prize for being the most un-guessed guest?'

He laughed. 'I should have thought of that.'

'I think you have thought of just about everything else. I should have come as a Roman—the Ides of March, of course.'

'No, not at all. I thought the invitation was pretty clear.' He gave me a stern look.

Bugger it! I hadn't read the invitation. Had I given myself away?

Gibson continued. 'Anyway, the idea was, come as anything that takes your fancy. And talking of fancy, where is your beautiful Marie Antoinette?'

'She's run off on me. Joan of Arc took me dancing and Marie Antoinette must have got jealous.'

'I don't see her anywhere. Is she likely to be cavorting in the Forum?'

'Quite likely,' I said. I knew that the champagne I had consumed had lessened my guard and that I was probably being too chatty. But then if I was stiff and silent, that could arouse worse suspicion.

'Ah, there she is,' said Gibson. We watched Stephanie descend the stairs. Gibson took off and cornered her. Next thing, they were dancing.

And then I froze. The Roman centurion coming towards me with a tray of drinks was Vesalik. He pushed the tray of drinks under my nose. I waved him away. I wanted to kill him and it was hard to keep control.

It was nearly an hour before I got Stephanie alone. By this time, the party had really taken off. A few people were splashing around in the pool and the music had taken on a Middle Eastern beat. Already there were several signs of inebriation. Joan of Arc was doing a belly dance and Spiderman was doing his best to climb the walls.

'Where have you been?' I hissed.

'Where have *you* been? You're supposed to be showing me the house layout,' she sniffed. 'You've been drinking,' she accused.

'I'm okay.'

'That's what they all say.' Stephanie glanced around to make sure we couldn't be heard. 'There were no locked rooms upstairs. There's only one locked door in the entire house. It's down the hallway, second on the left,' she whispered.

'That's Gibson's study,' I said.

'There are people hanging around the hallway. I haven't had a chance to try my keys.'

'Have you noticed there are at least three Caesars?' I asked.

'So?'

'That could be confusing if one goes missing.'

'Your job is to keep an eye on Gibson and Shelly—and no more grog! I'll see if the hallway is clear now.'

Stephanie left and I wandered out to the pool area. I was feeling hot in my heavy outfit and needed some air. A pleasant breeze helped cool me down. I was feeling envious of the people in the pool when I felt a touch at my elbow. Beside me was a very attractive Cleopatra. 'All alone, Your Majesty?' she smiled. 'Not for long I hope, *Your* Majesty.' I was enjoying the role-play. The gold mask she wore was tiny, barely covering her eyes. Her long, gleaming black hair with a straight fringe looked incredibly authentic. On her head was a small golden crown with a snake coiling upwards. Matching bands decorated each arm and gold coin earrings dropped almost to her shoulders. She wore a tight strapless gold top and sheer, gold billowing pants. Strappy gold sandals completed the outfit. She looked stunning.

'A great party, don't you think?' she asked.

'Yes, and a great house,' I said casting my eyes around the room.

'It has everything that opens and shuts.' She put

her hand to her mouth and whispered. 'Even a secret passage.'

'You're kidding.'

'Come, I'll show you.' We walked back inside the house. The entire back wall of the room was covered with Roman scenery. Cleopatra slipped behind the scenery into a space between the fake wall and the bookcase wall. I followed her. 'Now let me see. It was a Shakespeare if I remember right.' She rifled through the Shakespeare section. 'Macbeth? No. Here we are, A Midsummer's Night Dream.'

She removed the book and pressed the wall behind it. The library sprang into motion. Part of the wall opened up. I was amazed.

'Just like in the movies,' I said.

She replaced the book and walked through the opening. I followed her into a dark, narrow passage. The door swung closed behind us and a light came on. The passage went a short distance, then turned a corner and led to a door. 'That's Lance's office,' said Cleopatra.

'Why the passage?' I whispered as I tried the door. It was locked.

'Haven't a clue.'

'How did you find out about it?'

'Lance showed it to me. We were having a 'thing'. That was before Shelly came along.' Cleopatra started back and I followed. In the middle of the blank wall was a button. She pressed it and the wall swung open. We entered back into the living room and the door closed behind us.

The band was now playing a popular dance

number. 'Let's dance,' she said. I saw Stephanie heading towards us. 'I think I promised this one to Marie Antoinette.'

'Okay, later perhaps, at midnight. I want to see behind that mask,' she said flirtingly.

'See you at midnight, Cleo.'

Stephanie was looking frustrated. 'I still haven't had a chance to get into the study. There are people all over the place.'

'I'll get you in. Follow me.' I led Stephanie to the bookcase and within a minute we were outside the study door. 'This is another entrance to Gibson's study.' I said.

'How did you find this?'

'Let's say a certain Egyptian queen told me.'

'You sure it's the study?'

'That's what Cleo said. Got your keys?'

Stephanie pulled the bunch of keys from her skirt pocket. The first one failed but the second turned the lock. She smiled triumphantly.

'See, I was worth bringing, wasn't I?' I'll stand outside and keep watch.'

'Thanks.' Stephanie threw me a grateful smile as she pushed the door open.

'Just press the button on the wall when you want to get out.'

Back in the main room I kept watch. Gibson was mingling with the guests. Shelly was at the other end of the room talking to a guy in a Phantom of the Opera outfit. They seemed to be having a heated row. She was throwing her hands around and he was aggressively pointing his finger at her. Shelly stormed away from him and I lost sight of her.

The Phantom grabbed a drink from a passing Roman centurion and wandered out to the pool area. Most of the guests had gone outside. I was alarmed to see Joan of Arc staggering across the room towards me. I ducked behind the fake wall. At the other end, a nun was doing naughty things with a warlock. I was relieved to see Samson sneak up behind Joan, pick her up, and carry her out to the pool.

Food was being brought out to the pool area. I was feeling hungry and wandered out. I kept my eyes on the wall as I helped myself to a leg of chicken and a smoked salmon crepe. I then headed back to my post.

Nearly an hour went by and I went back to the passage. The study door was locked.

'Are you there, Stephanie?' I called softly. There was no answer. I went back to the big room and then down the hallway to the main study door and knocked. A Roman centurion approached. 'Can I help you, sir?'

'I'm looking for the bathroom,' I lied.

'Two doors down on your left, sir.'

I entered the bathroom and decided I might as well take a leak while I was there. I then went out to the pool and searched around. There was no sign of Stephanie. I took out my mobile and called her number. No answer. Now I was really worried. I needed help and walked out to the front gate. The guard was still on watch.

'I live down the road. I'm just off to check on the

kids. My wife's got the invitation. I won't need it to get back in, will I, mate?'

'No, go for it. I'll remember ya.'

Tanner's car was still parked in the same spot. He was asleep when I got there. I opened the driver's door and shook him. 'Stephanie's disappeared,' I muttered. Tanner came to life quickly. 'What do you mean, disappeared?'

'Just that. She got into Gibson's office and I haven't seen her since. She could be in trouble. You'd better get some assistance.'

'I've gotta check it out myself before I go starting a ruckus.'

'Okay. I'll show you where she went.'

We walked back to the house. 'How will you get past the guy at the gate?' I asked.

'I'll show my badge and say I'm investigating a noise complaint. You go in first. I don't think we should look like we know each other. I'll give you a couple of minutes before I follow.'

'I'll meet you at the fake Roman wall on the southern side of the main room,' I said as I walked ahead.

I saluted the guy at the gate.

'Kids okay?' he asked.

'Sound asleep.'

I entered the house and made for the appointed spot. Thirty minutes went by but Tanner didn't show. I decided he must have misunderstood my message and I wandered out to the pool area.

Here the party was really taking off. People were

splashing around in the water. Some had discarded their costumes and I was amused to see a lot of naked bodies with masked faces. The music had taken on an oriental beat and people were gyrating to the rhythm. Then the band seemed to reach a crescendo and people were counting—one, two, three, four, five, six, seven, eight, nine, ten, eleven, twelve! The drummer did a drum roll and hit the cymbals.

I suddenly realised it was midnight. A hand at my elbow reached up and grabbed my mask, pulling it off. I turned around and there was Cleopatra.

She grinned. 'I'm here as promised, Louis.' And then I saw Shelly, heading towards us. I grabbed Cleo around the waist, and together we jumped into the pool. As we plunged down together, the coloured bubbles fizzed around us. I felt my wig come off and I saw my moustache floating away. When we surfaced, I was still holding Cleopatra. Shelly was looking down at us. Cleo's face was partly hiding mine. I pulled her to me and gave her a long, lingering kiss. In the corner of my eye, I saw Shelly walk off. Cleo looked at me. 'God, without the mo and silver curls, you are just something.'

We were in the deep end of the pool, so I asked: 'Can you swim?'

'Of course,' she replied.

With that, I released my hold on her and swam off to the side. 'Catch up later, Cleo,' I called.

Shelly hadn't seen my face but I knew that without my mask, I was in danger. I hurried back to the main room, hoping to find Tanner. But instead, I saw Gibson and a centurion in the garden, heading towards the garage.  Minutes later, a black Porsche roared out into the driveway. Then I saw the Phantom.  He appeared from behind a bush and walked quickly back to the house.  I ran to my car and followed the Porsche.

As I followed the car along McCarrs Creek Road, I started shivering. The heavy brocaded coat was clinging to me and I was soaked through.

Eventually, the Porsche left the main road and turned into a long dark street towards Cottage Point and the waters of the Hawkesbury River.

Gibson stopped at the bottom of the street.  I parked halfway down the road, killed my headlights, and pulled off the heavy wet coat.

Gibson left the car carrying two bags and disappeared into a boathouse fronting the river.  Minutes later, a boat pulled away from the jetty.

I took out my mobile but it had been drenched in the pool, and wasn't transmitting.  So, I drove on home. Here, I again called Stephanie's mobile, and once again, nothing.  I tried her regular number at headquarters. Lockwood answered.  I told him the full story and was told to stay put.  I pulled off the rest of the Louis outfit and had a hot shower.

At four in the morning, I answered the door to Lockwood and another officer. I went through the whole series of events again, including what I had seen at Cottage Point.  They listened attentively and then Lockwood spoke.  'We found Detective Tanner lying unconscious in a street not far from the Gibson house.'

'How is he?'

'He's awake.  He said he entered the property and

was walking up the pathway to the house but remembers nothing after that.'

'And Stephanie?'

'We searched the house and the grounds. We've interviewed the guests who were still at the party, but there's no sign of her. We couldn't locate Lance Gibson either.'

'I'm not surprised. He took off in a boat, remember?'

Lockwood ignored my sarcasm and spoke again. 'We'll be interviewing all remaining guests tomorrow. We will probably want to talk to you again.'

'What did Shelly Gibson have to say?' I asked.

'That's police information,' Lockwood said curtly.

I shrugged and showed them out. I fell into bed and into a deep, troubled sleep. I woke at midday.

# CHAPTER 15
## *Brett*

I hung the wet Louis costume out to dry and then called Stephanie's mobile. It was still dead. I then drove up to the Gibson house and found it cordoned off. So, with nothing else to do, I picked up the Louis outfit and headed out to the costume hire place. The same sulky salesgirl laid it across the counter and fixed me with a petulant expression. 'The wig's missing,' she whined.

'Yes, I lost it,' I said.

'And where's the Marie Antoinette?'

'I lost that too.'

'Some wild party! You'll have to pay for it all, you know.'

'How much?'

'The wig's worth $50 and Marie Antoinette is $500. You gave us a deposit of $500 and the hiring fees were $50 each. So, you owe us $150.' I got out my credit card and handed it over. Just then I became aware of a presence beside me.

'Hi, Louis.'

I turned and looked into the clear blue eyes of a beautiful doll-like creature. It took some time for me to recognise her. It was Cleo. The black straight hair was now a pile of blond curls. Her perfect features were set into peachy skin that had never seen the sun. She was dressed in a pink silk top over a soft, swirling pink skirt. She handed a plastic bag to the salesgirl who emptied the Cleopatra outfit onto the counter and started going through it.

'You left me high and dry. Or should I say, low and wet! Where did you get to?' she said.

'I'm sorry. I was on a mission.'

'You missed the fun. The police were crawling all over the place for ages.' The salesgirl handed Cleo some money and stood nearby listening to us. 'What was your mission?' asked Cleo.

I took her arm and steered her to the front door of the shop. 'I was trying to find a murderer and now I am trying to find Marie Antoinette, who is really a police detective.'

'Wow. So, you're involved in all this. 'Are you a policeman?'

'No.'

Then how come you're involved?'

'I was helping Detective Darrieux with a case.'

Cleo's eyes were bright with excitement. 'Did the case involve Lance?'

'I think so.'

We started walking to our cars. I decided I should find out more from Cleo. She had had an association with Gibson and maybe could throw some light.

'I'm off to Cottage Point, like to come?' I asked.

'Am I safe? You won't dunk me in the water

again?'

'You're safe. And I'm sorry about the dunking.'

'What about the kiss? Are you sorry about that too?'

'Not at all. Are you?'

She shook her head. 'I rather liked it, Louis.'

'You'll have to stop calling me Louis. It makes me feel like a fly.' I grinned, recalling the popular fly-spray commercial featuring "Louis the Fly". 'It's Brett—Brett Carlton.'

'Tania Townsend. But I quite like Cleo.'

'Then I'll keep calling you Cleo.' I opened the passenger door and Cleo slid in. We drove in silence for a while. 'How did you meet Gibson?' I asked.

'He had just bought the house in Church Point and wanted an interior decorator. He found me in the local Pink Pages. I was so excited when I first walked into that house. It had awesome promise. I knew I could do wonders with it, I could turn it into a dream home—but that didn't happen. Lance had his own ideas. To this day, I don't know why he thought he needed a decorator. He opposed everything I suggested. I wanted to put light Roman blinds on the windows. But no! Lance wanted drapes.

The only thing he agreed to was ripping up the carpet and featuring the floorboards. They were in great condition, just needed a light sand and polish. I suggested cream shag rugs. But, oh no! Lance had a couple of big Persian rugs and he wanted to use those. And then he insisted that the drapes should match the rugs. He followed this dark, dreary theme throughout the entire house,' Cleo sighed.

'And your relationship took off during that time?'

'Yes. Lance used to open a bottle of champagne when I came over.  Then he asked me out to dinner and then he asked me to move in with him.'

'Did you?'

'No, I didn't feel enough for him, and I couldn't stand the house.  I hated the dark, creepy atmosphere.'

'But you had a relationship?'

'Yes.  He took me out to nice dinners.'

'Did you go out on his cruiser?'

'Golden Girl?   Oh yes.  I loved that.'

'Where did you go?'

'Just around the harbour.  He always took crew. He liked to relax and drink.'

'Did you ever notice anything unusual when you were on board?'

'Like what?'

'Anything unusual.' I repeated.

'No, but a couple of times some official-looking people boarded after we berthed.   Both times Lance sent me off and told me to wait in the coffee shop. I asked him who they were.  He wouldn't say, and he'd be quiet and grumpy after.'

'And when did Shelly hit the scene?'

'About six months after I first met Lance.  He phoned me one day and said an old girlfriend had fronted on his doorstep and was moving in.'

'How did you feel about that?'

'I didn't care.  The relationship had run its race and as I said, I'd never really loved Lance.'  Cleo's voice waivered as she spoke.  Recalling the events was obviously causing her distress.

'I had to go to the house to pick up some things I'd left there.  Shelly met me at the door.  I told her what I was there for.  She gave me a filthy look, got my stuff, threw it at me, and slammed the door in my face.  Shelly was a bitch.  She hated me.'  Cleo picked nervously at the skin near her thumbnail. There was a short silence and then she spoke again.

'I met Shelly a few times at the beautician's and she made a fool of me in front of everyone.  And then she damaged my car.'

'How?'

'She backed her big Pajero into the side of my Corolla. I was coming back from the shops and caught her doing it.  I yelled and said I'd get the police.  She laughed and said there were no witnesses and it was only my word against hers.  She said she would win because she had money and I didn't.'

'Did you report her?' I asked.

'Oh yes.  The police came around and looked at my car.  I got a call the next day to say they couldn't find any evidence that her car was responsible.  She was right—money talks.'

We drove on for a while and then I said, 'I'm surprised you got invited to the party.'

'So was I.  But I soon found out why.  Lance was inviting just about everyone he knew.  He wanted it to be the party of the year.  I decided to go out of curiosity.'

We drove the rest of the way in silence.  I found the street in Cottage Point and parked outside the boatshed.  There was a boat berthed at the jetty and a man was on board hammering nails into the boat's panels.

'What are we here for,' Cleo asked.

'I'm here to see a man about a boat,' I quipped.

We wandered into the boatshed and out to the jetty. The man on the boat was brown, scrawny, and silver-haired.  He looked up as we approached.

'Good day,' I called.

'G'day,' he replied.  I walked up to the boat. 'Do you know who owns this jetty?' I asked.

'I own it.'

'Oh, then was your boat berthed here on Saturday night, between midnight and one?'

The man screwed up his eyes and thrust out his lips. 'Are you from the cops?' he asked. Without waiting for an answer, he continued.  'I told you guys this morning. People use my jetty illegally.  I don't know who was here Saturday night.  They come and go all hours of the day and night. I live two streets away. I can't be here all the time watching.  I run an honest business, and I don't own a boat.'

'What exactly is your business, sir?'

'I repair boats.  People leave their boats here and I do minor repairs for them, mostly carpentry and stuff.  I don't charge much and I pay my taxes,' he said gruffly as he turned back to his hammering.

Cleo and I walked to the car.  'Feel like something to eat?' I asked.

'I guess so.  Come to think of it, I haven't eaten all day.'

'Nor have I.'

We drove to the nearby Cottage Inn. It was now nearly five and the restaurant was empty apart from a few late lunch customers. We found a good table looking out onto the river and ordered prawn cutlets.

The waiter poured our wine. I watched Cleo as she sipped hers. She had an uncanny resemblance to Crystal and I felt myself warming to her. 'What happened after I left the party?' I asked.

'After being dunked in the pool, I needed to check my make-up. I'd left my bag in the upstairs bedroom. So, I went up there, but the door was locked. I went back to the party and someone asked me to dance.'

'Did you see Shelly?' I asked.

'I think she was around. But Lance seemed to disappear. And then there was a big commotion. They found that policeman in the street outside. An ambulance came and then police were everywhere.'

'Did the police question you?'

'Yes. I didn't have much to tell them, but they took my details and said they'd be calling me. I told them I couldn't get my bag as the door to the main bedroom was locked. The policeman said they had been upstairs and none of the rooms were locked. I went up. Sure enough, the door was wide open and my bag was sitting on the chair.'

'Did you notice anything unusual about the room? Did it look the same as before?'

'Yes. I think so.' Cleo thought for a few seconds and then looked at me with her eyes wide. 'There was a funny smell.'

'What do you mean, funny?'

'It was a smell that made me feel frightened. I wanted to get out of there as quickly as I could.'

'Try to remember the smell, Cleo.'

She frowned and closed her eyes tightly. 'It was a smell I recognised.' She smiled as the answer came to her. 'Yes, I remember. I was about fifteen and invited to my first real party. There were kids from higher grades there. A group of them were out in the yard. I went out to take a look, see what was going on. Just before I got there, they took off running in all directions. Then I saw a girl lying on the ground. I went over to see if she was okay. She was so pale and still. And then I smelled this awful smell. I ran inside to get help. I found out later what had happened. The kids were experimenting with stuff they'd stolen from the school lab. They were using ether. That smell was ether.'

I drew in my breath. Had Stephanie been imprisoned in this room and then knocked out with ether? I thought for a while and then asked: 'Cleo, is there a staircase leading from the upstairs, other than the one leading into the main room?'

'Yes. There's a small balcony off the main bedroom. A staircase runs down to the back garden.'

I ordered another bottle of wine and we stayed at the restaurant until after nine. I drove back to the fancy-dress shop.

'Do you have a phone number?' I asked. She fished in her bag and handed me a card. '

Do *you* have a phone number?' she mimicked me. I handed her my card. I kissed her and said, 'I'll call you.' She slipped out of my car and walked toward hers.

When I got home, I turned on the television. Already Stephanie's disappearance and Tanner's attack had hit the media.

# CHAPTER 16
## *Brett*

The next day all the television channels were reporting the events at Church Point. Around midday, I answered the door to Lockwood and another guy who introduced himself as Detective Inspector Dennis Randall. I took them into the living room.

Randall bore into me with his small brown eyes. 'Lance Gibson has turned up at the house. He denies ever going off in a boat on Friday night and claims he drove a sick guest home from his party. He claims he stayed the night at the guest's house and also all day, Saturday. He wasn't aware that he was wanted until he saw the news on television this morning.'

'That's crap. Surely you don't believe any of it!'

'We have interviewed the sick guest and he has supported everything Gibson said.'

'Apart from the fact that I know it's a load of shit, it doesn't make sense. Why would Gibson run out on his own party just to drive a guest home, and then stay away for nearly two days?'

'He claims he felt tired and decided to take a short nap. He says he slept all that night and most of the next day.'

'Who is this witness?' I asked scornfully.

'An employee of Mr Gibson's.'

'That figures,' I muttered cynically.

'It's their word against yours,' Randall said stiffly.

'I told you the truth.'

Randall narrowed his eyes. 'We've checked out the boatshed and jetty at Cottage Point. We can't find any witnesses to support your account of a boat taking off soon after midnight.' Randall walked to the window. He spoke again with his back to me. 'You stated that you followed Lance Gibson to a jetty in Cottage Point and saw him boarding a boat which took off minutes later. '

'Yes.'

'The other man didn't board?'

'No, he stayed in the car.'

'Do you know who the other man was?'

'He was dressed as a Roman centurion, like all the waiters at the party. I only know it wasn't Bruno Vesalik. This guy was a lot smaller than Vesalik.'

'You said Gibson carried some bags on board. What kind of bags?'

'Two suitcases.'

'Please describe the car.'

'It was a late model black Porsche.'

'The Gibsons don't own such a car.'

'I know.'

Randall wore an inscrutable expression. 'You're sure Mrs Gibson wasn't in the car?'

'Not unless she was in the boot.'

'This isn't a joking matter, Mr Carlton.'

'I'm not joking. Shelly Gibson was still at the party when Gibson left.'

'You're sure?'

'Positive. What did Shelly Gibson have to say?'

'She claims she was at the party the entire night. Can you back that up?'

'I saw her early in the night and then again at midnight. Where she was in between...I have no idea.'

'One of the guests seemed to remember seeing a person dressed as Marie Antoinette walking up the stairs. He wasn't clear on the time but was certain it was before midnight. She was with another woman,' said Randall.

'There was another Marie Antoinette at the party.'

'Yes. we talked to those people. They weren't enjoying the party and apparently left before ten. The woman claims she never went upstairs.'

Randall turned away from the window. His expression was solemn. 'I need to know more about your involvement. I understand you accompanied Detective Darrieux to the party. How come?'

'As I'm sure you know, Detective Darrieux was investigating the murder of a girl three years ago. The Gibsons were involved in this matter. Detective Darrieux needed to gain access to the Gibson house to make some... inquiries. She decided to go to the party in disguise.'

'She could have applied for a warrant.'

'She obviously felt she didn't have the necessary criteria to apply for a warrant.'

'Then why did she take you and not a police

officer?'

'She knew I was familiar with the house'.

'Is that all?' His voice was harsh. He didn't wait for an answer. 'If what you are saying is true, then Detective Darrieux broke a fundamental police rule. She should not have involved a private citizen in her investigation, nor should she have gone into a dangerous situation without backup.'

'She had Tanner.'

'Tanner was outside the grounds—hardly a backup,' he muttered sarcastically. 'We have now interviewed every person on the guest list. Apparently, everyone attended except for Mr and Mrs Conte who claim they never received an invitation.'

'Tanner somehow got their invitation. We used it to get in,' I said.

Randall frowned. 'It appears there was a lot of alcohol consumed, and none of the guests seem to be able to shed much light on anything.' He walked back to the window and gazed out at the ocean. I couldn't see the expression on his face but his voice was stern.

'Tell me what happened from the time you and Detective Darrieux first entered the house and when you last saw her.'

I went through the whole set of events while Randall stood with his back to me, listening. There was a long silence. He finally turned and spoke. 'When you were keeping guard on the secret passage, did you observe anything unusual?'

'Well, the whole scene was rather unusual. There were a hundred people all dressed up like someone else, all wearing masks. That in itself is unusual.'

'I think you know what I mean, Mr. Carlton.'

'I saw a guy dressed as the Phantom. He seemed to be arguing with Mrs Gibson.'

'And?'

'That's all. Nothing seemed to come of it. But later I saw the Phantom guy in the garden around the time Gibson took off in the Porsche.'

'Were you in view of the internal staircase when you were guarding the secret passage?'

'No. I couldn't see the staircase.'

'One of the guests took photos during the night. She took quite a few before and after midnight.' Randall walked to the dining table, took an envelope out of his pocket, and spread some photos around the table. 'Do you know this man?' He selected a photo and handed it to me. The man was wearing the Phantom cloak but now his mask was off. It was Rick Bradshaw. I told Randall about Rick Bradshaw's connection with Crystal and felt from Randall's expression, he already knew.

'Anything else you can add?' Randall asked.

'Yes. Tania Townsend went up to the main bedroom to get her bag. She noticed a smell in the room, a smell of ether.'

'My investigating officers didn't say anything about an ether smell,' said Randall.

'Well, I think it's possible that Stephanie Darrieux was imprisoned in that room and subjected to ether. There's a balcony with stairs leading off the room. She could have been carried down the stairs and—God only knows what happened!' I whispered.

Randall's mobile went off. 'Excuse me,' he said as he answered it. His expression turned grim and stony as he listened, 'Where? Definitely identified?' There was another pause and then he spoke again. 'Shit! I'll be at headquarters within an hour. But keep a watch on the Gibson place.' He closed his phone and looked first at Lockwood and then me. 'Detective Darrieux has been found.'

'How is she?' I asked.

'I'm afraid she's dead. Her body was found by some fishermen at the mouth of the river a short time ago.'

I slumped into a chair and put my hands to my head. I felt numb, just the way I'd felt when Danni told me that Crystal had been found. 'What happened?'

Two fishermen saw what looked like a wig floating. They remembered what they'd seen on television about the missing detective wearing a costume and wig. They picked up the wig and called Triple 0. Police divers went down and found the body.'

'How did she die?' I asked.

'I fear we have a psychopath on the loose. Detective Darrieux's throat was cut and her face was mutilated.'

'What sort of monster would do that?' I said half to myself as I remembered Stephanie's iridescent green eyes and her perfect oval face. I thought of our date at Jericho's and how beautiful she was.

Randall, followed by Lockwood walked to the door. 'Please do not leave Sydney,' he muttered as they left.

I remained in my chair. Gradually the numbness in my body dissipated, only to be replaced by a familiar and frightening sensation. I knew the symptoms. The spiralling was starting and I had to stop it before it took hold. I had to stay out of that black hole. It had imprisoned me once and I couldn't let it happen again. I took out one of Gene's tapes and tuned into his gentle voice.

An hour or so later, I opened the door to Steve. He had seen the news and wanted to find out more. I gave him a beer and told him the story.

'It's like something out of the movies,' he said.

'I wish it was a movie. That lovely girl didn't deserve to die like that.' My eyes started to fill.

Steve put his hand on my shoulder. 'Do you think it's someone we know?'

'Rick Bradshaw was at the party. As far as we know, he hardly knew Shelly or Gibson. What was he doing there?'

I told Steve about the incident between Bradshaw and Shelly at the party. 'What was going on between them, do you think?' he asked.

'I don't know but they both looked fit to kill each other.' We sat in silence for a while.

I spoke again. 'When Crystal started seeing Bradshaw, she must have been working with Jaz. Had Jaz met him before your birthday party?'

'I think she met him once before.'

'What was her impression?'

'Crystal told Jaz that Rick was very possessive. I remember Jaz thinking it was odd Crystal didn't want

Rick to know when she and her mother had lunch together. She said Rick would be jealous. He wanted Crystal all to himself.'

'Weird. I'm certain Bradshaw has something to hide. But the police don't seem to be treating him like a suspect. I'd like to know a bit more about Mr Rick Bradshaw but I'm afraid he and I are not exactly on friendly terms.'

'Why don't I go around and have a talk to him?' asked Steve.

'What would you say?'

'I could say I was pretty amazed at the goings-on at the Gibson's place, that sort of thing. See what he has to say. It might press a button.'

'Do you think he could get suspicious?' I asked.

'I don't think so. We kept in touch with him for a few months after Crystal's disappearance.'

My mind was working overtime. 'Steve, if I showed you how to plant a bugging device, would you fix one at Bradshaw's place?'

Steve's grin told me he would be only too happy to help out. As Bradshaw lived alone, the logical place for a bug would be near his telephone. I showed Steve the device and how to fix it. 'I think it's important that we do this as early as possible.' I looked at my watch. It was now nearly six. 'Could you go around tonight?'

Steve left and I suddenly thought of Champ. I grabbed some mince out of the fridge and drove to Stephanie's aunt's house. The place was in darkness. Champ greeted me at the side gate and I patted him.

'Hi Champ. I'll bet you're hungry'.

He followed me with his tail wagging frantically. I found two dishes on the back deck, filled one with water, and shovelled the meat into the other one.

Steve phoned around ten that night and gleefully told me that the device was in place under the telephone table. 'It was easy. I pretended I needed to call Jaz and had mislaid my mobile. Rick gave me a clear go at the phone.'

'Did you ask him about the party?' I asked.

'I talked about the party but he didn't say anything about being there. In fact, he said he hadn't seen the Gibsons since the memorial service.'

'That shows he's lying. I'll be listening with eager ears to the bastard's phone talks,' I grunted.

The next morning, I set up in the street at the back of Bradshaw's house. It was just after seven. I waited patiently. Then around nine, Bradshaw called a number. My device could only pick up his voice and I was unable to hear the other party. Bradshaw spoke.

'It's Rick Bradshaw. Yeah, well, you ran out on me. I waited two hours. Don't think you can just fob me off!' There were a few seconds of silence and Bradshaw spoke again. 'Well, my price has gone up. If you want me to keep quiet and give you the stuff, it'll cost you a million. The woman cop has turned up murdered.

So that's two now.' There was a long silence before Bradshaw spoke again. 'I don't buy that crap. I'll give you twelve hours. I'll come around at nine tonight. You better have it, or I go to the cops.' There was another pause. 'Hang on. I'll get a pencil.' Bradshaw said irritably. 'Now where's this boat house? '

crystal

Another pause 'Okay.    I'll be there at nine
tonight—and no tricks!'
So, Rick Bradshaw was blackmailing someone.
He was meeting that person at nine tonight at a boat
house.  Was it the boathouse at Cottage Point?  I
decided that I would follow Bradshaw and let him lead
me to this mysterious person who apparently has lots to
hide.
That afternoon I cycled down to the beach.   The
glorious feeling of the salt water bubbling over me had a
therapeutic effect.  I surfed until I was exhausted and
then headed home.

*

I set out at seven and parked across from
Bradshaw's house.    It was dark when his car backed
down the driveway and out onto the street.  I followed at
a distance.  Sure enough, he was on his way to Cottage
Point.  On the way, I called Lockwood's number and got
the answering machine. I left a message saying where I
was going and who I was following.
When I got there, I saw Bradshaw's car parked at
the bottom of the street.  Another car was nearby.  I
parked halfway down, and keeping in the shadows,
walked towards the boatshed.  As I approached it, I
heard voices.  I crept up to a window and peered in.
Bradshaw was there talking to someone.  I moved closer
to the doorway.
'Now where's my dough?' shouted Bradshaw.  I
peered into the dimly lit room.  A figure dressed in a black
hooded jacket stood with its back turned to me.
'Here's the money.  You can count it,' said the

person. I immediately recognised the voice. It was Shelly's.

'Where is the paperwork you promised?' she said, handing Bradshaw a fat parcel.

He flicked through large wads of $100 notes.

'It's in my car,' he muttered.

'Get it. Leave the money here,' she said. I stiffened as I saw Bradshaw coming towards me and pulled back into the shadows. Bradshaw walked past and headed for his car.

Then a vice-like grip encircled my neck. 'Now, what have we here?' said a husky voice. Hot, fetid breath almost suffocated me as the grip tightened. I tried to break free but was no match for Bruno Vesalik. He dragged me into the boat shed keeping his hold on my neck. Shelly looked up surprised. 'Brett!'

'What are you up to, Shelly?'

She fixed me with a lopsided grin. 'What do you think?'

'I know that Bradshaw's blackmailing you and I know that it's connected with Stephanie Darrieux.'

Rick Bradshaw entered. His eyes glared when he saw me. 'What's he doing here?' he snarled. Vesalik's grip around my neck tightened.

'Let's say he's an uninvited guest. Now, where's that stuff you promised me?' Bradshaw handed an envelope to Shelly. She quickly looked through the contents. 'It's all there,' said Bradshaw.

'So I see.'

'What are you going to do about him?' Bradshaw asked, glaring at me.

'He won't be causing any trouble.'

'Good.  Now, where's my money.'

'I'm curious to know, Rick, just why you didn't spill everything three years ago?  You knew my identity then.'

'Yes.  Crystal told me about you when we were in bed that last night.  How you had changed your face and how you were signalling the other cruiser.  It sounded like one of her delusions.  Crystal would see people who weren't there and she heard voices.  I thought the story she told me that night was just a delusion.  When they found the empty dinghy, I thought she'd killed herself. But when her body was found and the cops said it was murder, I knew then that Crystal had told me the truth.  I knew you'd killed her.  I wanted to kill *you*.  But I decided to take your money instead.'

'Why didn't you tell the police about Crystal's problem?' I asked trying to shake off Vesalik's grip.

'I loved Crystal.  I didn't want her memory tarnished.  It wasn't anyone's business.'

As Rick spoke, I realised something about myself. I too knew Crystal had a problem. It was obvious when she spoke about seeing Hannah Edwards. Yet I didn't mention this to anyone and chose to forget it. Maybe like Rick, I was protecting Crystal's image.

'How did you get these papers and photos?' Shelly held up the package.

'Well, your trusted cleaner isn't so trustworthy after all.  I made it my business to set up a friendship with her.  She was a lonely old girl and fell for my line.  She found your medical records with the before and after photos.

'The bitch,' snarled Shelly.

'She won't need to clean anymore after I give her a share of the money. Now, where is it?'

Shelly dug into her duffle bag. My body prickled when I saw the gun in her hand. With her free hand, she withdrew a length of rope from the bag.

'Tie them up.' She tossed the rope to Vesalik. He caught it and pushed me to the floor. His massive foot pinned me down as he cut the rope into four lengths. My struggling was no match for his brute strength and my hands were tied securely behind my back in less than a minute.

'You really thought you could blackmail me, did you, Rick?' Shelly asked.

'Bitch! I should have dobbed you in, see you rot in jail.'

Vesalik finished tying my feet together and was slowly rising when Bradshaw jumped him with a karate kick to the chin. Taken by surprise, Vesalik stumbled back, lost his balance and hit the floor with a heavy thud. Bradshaw then turned his attention to Shelly and walked towards her with arms outstretched. There was a shot, and then another. The noise reverberated around the boat shed leaving a faint echo behind. Rick Bradshaw lay on the ground. His eyes were wide open. Blood oozed from a hole in the side of his forehead. Vesalik slowly got to his feet and stumbled to where Bradshaw lay.

'He's dead,' he grunted.

My heart was pounding. 'You killed him,' I whispered hoarsely.

She ignored me and spoke to Vesalik. 'Get the ring off his finger and check his pockets. We don't want any identification.' Vesalik pulled the ring off Bradshaw's finger and then pulled a set of keys and a wallet out of his coat pocket.

'Now the drums, Bunny,' said Shelly. Vesalik grinned, showing his crooked yellow teeth, and left the shed.

'We're going to have a little fire. You and Rick will be having early cremations.'

I was working my hands around, trying to loosen the rope. Vesalik had done a good job. The knot was unyielding. I noticed a nail sticking out of the floor close by. If I could only get to that, I might be able to wear the ropes loose.

Vesalik entered the shed carrying two big drums. He started splashing liquid around the inner walls. I smelled petrol and prayed that Lockwood had got my message. The boat shed would go up like tinder once a match fell, and it would be all over in a couple of minutes. I had to play for time. Shelly's need to brag might just buy me the time I needed.

'What did you do to Crystal?'

'Pretty Crystal. She caught me signalling the cruiser. She guessed it was a drugs heist.'

'So, the cruiser *was* following us. It *was* Lance Gibson.'

'Right. And the haul was big. Too big to risk losing. The coast guard was watching Golden Girl so we couldn't use her. A pleasure cruiser returning from a fun weekend wouldn't raise any suspicion. I organised the weekend cruise specifically to pick up the drugs. But then those stupid friends of yours had to insist on Crystal coming.'

'How did Crystal guess it was a drug deal?'

'She knew I was in the business.'

'How did she know?'

'You haven't guessed, have you?' she sneered. 'You don't know who I am, do you?'

I shook my head and gazed contemptuously at her twisted face.

'I'm Rachael, Rachael Livingstone,' she laughed crazily.

'But I've seen photos of Rachael...'

'Oh yes. That was me—then. But I had a makeover.' Shelly did a little pirouette before facing me again. She sneered: 'The ugly duckling became almost pretty. But never quite as pretty as Crystal or that woman cop.'

Shelly's mouth turned down at the corners. 'From the day I first saw Crystal, I hated her and her pretty face. When I started dealing at school, I decided that if I was busted, Crystal would cop the blame. I stored the stuff in her locker. The cops didn't believe either of us and we were both sent up. But I had the satisfaction of knowing that Crystal was copping it too.'

'Who were you working with?'

'Lance. It's always been Lance. I was buying my stuff from him when I was fourteen. When I was sprung, Lance promised if I kept quiet, he would give me fifty thousand when I got out. I didn't squeal. By that time, he had really gone ahead. He was direct dealing and making mega-bucks. He gave me the money and I spent it on plastic surgery.' Shelly looked around at Vesalik. He had almost completed his circle of the boatshed.

'How could surgery change your face so much?'

'The wonders of modern plastic surgery. The results were miraculous…new nose, new chin. For the first time in my life, I could look in the mirror. I threw away the glasses for contacts and had all my teeth capped. I dyed my hair blonde and worked out at the gym. Fixing my body took a lot less effort than fixing my face. It all took six months. After that, Rachael Livingstone disappeared from the face of the earth.'

'You were dealing when we met?' I asked.

'Yes. But I gave it up soon after. I stupidly thought I loved you, that I could have a normal life, a house, a garden, a nice car. But you stuffed it all up when you gave up your job. I knew I would never get the things I wanted. So, I called Lance.'

'That's what you were up to those three nights every week?'

'Yes. But it was hard work and I never really made enough.'

Vesalik came over to us. 'We gotta get out,' he croaked.

'Okay, okay. Keep your pants on, Bunny.'

'Tell me what happened on that last day.' I was guessing that Shelly would want to keep bragging. I was right. She launched into a full recollection of what had happened in the twenty-four hours from when she saw me with Crystal right up to the following afternoon.

I felt sick in the stomach as I listened to the

ghastly events. But I knew I had to keep playing for time, had to keep her talking.

'And what happened to Stephanie Darrieux?' I asked.

'You can thank Bradshaw for that. He came to the house a few days before the party—said he knew who I was. Crystal had told him that last night on the boat. He had my medical records, photos and birth certificate. He threatened to show these to the police if I didn't come good with $100,000. I told him I needed time to put the money together. He saw some party invitations lying around, grabbed one, and said he would see me at the party and I'd better have the money.' Shelly looked down at Bradshaw's body. 'The silly fool would have got his $100,000, only he got greedy.

'What has all that got to do with Stephanie Darrieux?' I asked.

'After he bailed me up at the party, I went to Lance's study to get the money from the safe. That's when I found your cop standing at the desk reading Lance's clipboard. I knew what was on that clipboard—all the details about the haul he was bringing in that night. She asked me about the drug running. I told her I didn't know anything about it, said I was innocent and would prove it by helping her get Lance's private papers.'

'Stephanie wouldn't have fallen for that.'

'But she did. I told her that all Lance's files and papers were in the upstairs safe and that I knew the combination. She came with me to the bedroom. I signalled Bunny on the way up the stairs. He followed, knocked her out, and stuffed a pad of ether over her face We took her down the back stairs to Bunny's car and drove to the jetty where the hired boat was moored.'

Vesalik was breathing heavily. I could see he was getting panicky. 'C'mon, let's get outta here,' he wheezed. But Shelly's need to brag propelled her on. She ignored Vesalik.

'I thought how pretty she looked in her Marie Antoinette outfit. Too pretty! So, I cut her throat and made a few little patterns on her face. I tied weights around her feet, took the boat out to the ocean, and dumped her. I was back at the party well before midnight.'

'You evil, insane bitch,' I hissed.

'Got your lighter, Bunny?' Her face was cold and hard.

'I'm not going to shoot you, Brett. I'll just let the flames do their work. Check him for ID and get his car keys.'

Vesalik leapt forward and felt in my pockets. I had left my wallet in my car. He found my keys and pulled my watch off. They walked to the doorway and Vesalik dropped the lighter.

Within seconds the flames were licking around the entire circumference of the shed. I bumped across to the nail and started feverishly rubbing the rope against it. The heat was growing and the flames rising. Smoke was filling my lungs. It seemed like an eternity before I cut through the first rope. But that was enough to allow me to free my hands. I tackled the ropes on my feet.

Vesalik hadn't done such a tight job and I had

them undone quickly. The entire shed was now a wall of fire. My lungs felt as if they were bursting. I said a silent prayer and tore through the flames.

Outside, I took in great gulps of air. Then I saw Shelly running back into the shed. She disappeared into the flames. Vesalik seemed to come from out of nowhere. He lunged at me with his knife raised. I felt weak from the restriction in my lungs and couldn't move. Then there was a loud bang. Vesalik's eyes widened as if he had just seen a ghost and he fell at my feet. Lockwood came running across.

'You took your time.' I muttered. Lockwood was shouting directions into his mobile. 'Yes, fire brigades and ambulance, High Street, Cottage Point.' He looked across at the inferno. 'Anyone inside?'

'Rick Bradshaw's inside but he doesn't need an ambulance.' I looked at the rising flames. 'Shelly Gibson's in there too. I don't think she'll need one either.'

'But you will. Look at your hands.' said Lockwood. I was then aware of a painful stinging sensation. I looked at my hands and felt my body start to shake. Yes, I needed an ambulance.

*

They took me to the hospital where I spent time in the burns unit. After a few days, I was moved to a private room. I watched a bit of television but mainly I just thought. I thought deeply about what Shelly had told me and also what Bradshaw had said just before he died. Steve and Jaz visited and filled in further details.

# CHAPTER 17
## *Brett*

Randall and Lockwood came the next day. 'How are you doing?' asked Randall.

'I think I'll live.'

'You got out in time. Another few seconds and—

'Why did Shelly Gibson run back into the fire?' I asked.

'She had left the money behind and went back for it.'

'Money was her idol. It killed her in the end.' I whispered. Randall and Lockwood hovered above me, both looking grim.

'But how did you find out about the money?' I asked.

'Bruno Vesalik told us.'

'But Vesalik's dead.' I glared at Lockwood. 'You shot him. He fell at my feet.'

'We shoot to apprehend, not to kill. Vesalik will recover and face his charges,' said Randall.

'What *are* his charges?'

'He confessed to drug running but says he had nothing to do with Detective Darrieux's death or Rick Bradshaw's.'

'Bullshit! He helped Shelly both times. And he was more than happy to see me go up in smoke.'

'He will be charged with your attempted murder and complicity in the other two deaths.'

'Good. What about Gibson?'

'We searched his house and found the stash he collected the night of the party. We've arrested him and charged him with illicit drug dealing, the attack on Tanner and complicity in Crystal Morgan's murder. He apparently played no part in Detective Darrieux's murder.'

'It's my fault she's dead. I suggested going to that party.'

'Stephanie had a mind of her own. She would have gone anyway. She was aware that Gibson knew his house and his boat were being watched. An elaborate masked party could mean only one thing. He was trying to create a diversion so he could slip out undetected. Stephanie knew there was danger.'

'How did Stephanie's parents take it?'

'Very badly. Their other child was murdered too.'

'I know.'

'We've uncovered some information about Crystal.'

I felt a shot of electricity shoot through me. I looked at Randall with raised eyebrows.

'It came to light when we were trying to find Bradshaw's next of kin. We started with the crowd he was working for. Apparently, he was a loner, no confidants there, not even a friend.' Randal paced to the small window and continued talking, facing away.

'So, we had to dig deeper, look somewhere else. His tax records told us he'd previously worked with...' Randall turned and eyeballed me. 'Corrective Services at Morrisset.'

'That's where Crystal did her time,' I murmured.

'Yes, and that's where he met her.'

'That would have been around nine years ago.'

'Exactly.' Randall moved back to my bedside. 'We visited the Centre and found that Bradshaw had confided in someone there, a guy named Alan Beaufort. Beaufort remembered Crystal, said Braithwaite took a special interest in her.'

'I'll bet he did,' I muttered scathingly.

'He became something of a mentor...protected her from the bullies, gave her special privileges. He was the one who put in the good word and recommended her sentence be reduced. He even called on her parents to check them out. Neither of them had visited Crystal, and that rang a few alarm bells. Well, he found them. They were still at the same house, but now both were advanced alcoholics and living in squaller. The house was a filthy mess. When Crystal was released, he took her back to his pad.'

'Totally illegal, I would think.'

'You think right. Bradshaw knew he couldn't stay with the Department, so after a few weeks, he put in his notice. He organized Crystal to finish her Graphic Design course and found himself a job in the city. When Crystal graduated, he got her a job in the same building as himself.

'Why didn't this all come out three years ago?'

'He gave the name of his current employer which was all correct, and the police didn't check any further. After all, back then, they weren't chasing a killer. It was a missing person, probably accidental death or at worst, suicide.

'According to Beaufort, Bradshaw became something of a Svengali to Crystal. He took total control over her. He became a father, lover and controller all rolled into one. It was the first time Crystal had ever experienced any sort of caring, and she responded to it.

'And the birthmother, Gabrielle?'

'She had been watching Crystal for years. But because she had signed something at the adoption, she obeyed the rules and kept her distance. When Marcy and John Ryan both died soon after Crystal's release, she turned up on Bradshaw's doorstep.

Being the ultimate controller, he ordered her off. But Crystal wanted to see her birthmother and she managed to contact her. They discovered a wonderful connection. Gabrielle would call into Crystal's office during lunch hour, and they'd go out for a meal and a chat. Although Bradshaw worked in the same building, he was with another company and Crystal was able to keep her meetings with Gabrielle a secret.'

'All this explains Crystal's relationship with Bradshaw,' I said wistfully as I remembered Crystal's almost subservient attitude.

Randall's forehead creased as he unzipped his briefcase and removed a bundle of papers. 'There's something else. We found these at Bradshaw's house.

He wrote a detailed account of events on the island.
This is a copy.' Randall dropped the papers onto my
bed. 'It won't be needed in either of the trials, so you
might be interested in reading it.'

\*

After the two police left, I lay for a long time,
thinking. Finally, I read Bradshaw's journal. It filled in all
the gaps and allowed me to understand all the events
that occurred on that fateful day three years ago. At last,
using Rick's notes, Shelly's confession in the boatshed,
the police report, Jaz and Steve's comments, and a
smattering of my own imagination, I was able to piece it
all together.

# CHAPTER 18
## *Brett*

When Shelly saw me leave the beach, she decided to follow. She had previously seen Crystal take the same track and suspected that we had arranged to meet. When she saw us together, she was seized with rage. Her first instinct was to confront and accuse us. But she decided against this. Tonight, was the big night. At all costs, there should be nothing to cause upheaval. She would deal with Crystal in her own time.

She returned to the beach and found Rick sitting alone, reading. Steve and Ben were splashing around in the water and Jaz and Danni were sitting near the dying barbeque, eating cakes. Shelly walked to the water's edge and sat. The outgoing tide lapped her feet. She was seething with hatred and rage.

After a short while, she saw Crystal return to the beach and sit down next to Rick. 'Hypocritical bitch,' Shelly muttered to herself. She sat staring at the water for nearly an hour. In all that time she was fantasising about how she would get even with Crystal.

Finally, she decided a bucket of acid in that pretty face would do the trick.

Steve and Ben came out of the water and started packing the dinghy. Shelly noted that there was still no sign of me. 'Want to come back now?' called Steve as Jaz and Danni boarded the dinghy. Shelly stood and waved them away. 'I'll go later,' she called.

She was surprised to see Crystal approaching her. What a nerve the bitch has. Crystal didn't notice Shelly's cold stare as she joined her at the water's edge. Crystal needed an answer to something that had bothered her for nearly forty-eight hours. Something only Shelly could explain.

'Shelly, I need to ask you something. I saw you signalling that big cruiser the first night out and I saw it signalling you back. What's that all about?'

Shelly was flummoxed by this question. It was the last thing she expected. 'You're quite wrong. I didn't signal anybody.'

'But I saw you.'

'You're a liar.' Shelly shouted those words at Crystal with hate and venom. Crystal blinked. She had heard that same voice using those same words before. She looked into Shelly's blazing eyes and was transported back in time. Back to when she had been summoned to Sister Monica's office.

She expected the summons to be connected with the swimming trials. They were coming up soon and Sister Monica always made sure that Crystal was prepared. She was surprised to see Rachael Livingstone standing before Sister Monica's desk. Maybe this had something to do with the bullying complaint.

Crystal had never seen Monica so stern and severe. It soon became clear that the summons had nothing to do with swimming or bullying, but something so serious and so traumatic that Crystal's life would be changed forever. She listened in disbelief as Rachael Livingstone accused her.

'There's nothing in my locker, but hers is full of the stuff,' Rachel accused.

Crystal tried to explain how the drugs got in her locker. 'Those packages are Rachael's. She said they were cosmetics.'

'You're a liar.' Rachael yelled and eyeballed her with those blazing eyes.

*

The same eyes Crystal was seeing now. Suddenly a veil was lifted, and in that instant, Crystal knew. She was with Rachael Livingstone and she was consumed by fear.

Shelly guessed by Crystal's wide-eyed expression, that she had finally guessed her identity. The whole plan for tonight would be destroyed if Crystal talked. She looked up and saw me arriving at the beach from the far end. She also saw Steve returning to shore in the dinghy. Crystal walked back to Rick. Eventually, everyone boarded the dinghy and within minutes we were on the boat.

Crystal was first in the shower. She let the hot water run over her and tried to think. Already she was feeling confused and frightened. She wanted to tell me about Shelly but that would mean telling me about her time in detention. It could spoil everything. Our

romance had just started. Instead, she decided to tell
Rick when they were alone in their cabin. She put on her
white shorts and pink top and then, as an afterthought,
her emerald bracelet. She wondered why she had
brought it. It was very valuable. In fact, she had emptied
her bank account to pay for it. But the fear of losing it
had stopped her from putting it on this weekend. As this
was the last night, she decided she might as well wear
it.

Shelly was next to shower. She came out wearing
her colourful caftan. Jaz and Danni admired it. They had
never seen Shelly dressed in anything so 'way-out'.

Around nine Danni set up the Ouija. Crystal was
not in favour of disturbing the spirit world but as Rick had
been so unsociable the whole weekend, she felt she
should go along with it.

Shelly, too, didn't want to cause any dissension.
As the night wore on, she had relaxed a little. Maybe
Crystal hadn't recognised her and maybe she wasn't
going to say anything about the signalling. She was still
consumed with hatred and anger but her plans for
retribution consoled her a little, and she was prepared to
wait her time.

Crystal sat at the table and joined hands with the
others. She believed the Ouija was dangerous and
hated being there. She watched the glass sliding
backward and forward and thought about Hannah
And when the Ouija hurtled to 'H' and then 'A' and then
to 'N', she was certain that Hannah was there.

She knew if she left the table, Hannah would
leave too.

*And then Shelly brought her the coffee.  This really terrified her.  After their words on the beach, it seemed weird that Shelly was actually doing something nice for her.  Maybe Shelly was trying to poison her.  Yes, that's it.  Shelly was trying to poison her.  But Crystal didn't know that her cup and everyone else's, contained not poison but a strong sedative.  There is no way I will drink that coffee, thought Crystal.  She placed it carefully on the table and pretending to trip, swept her hand against the cup, scattering its contents.  Crystal caught the livid look in Shelly's face.  Yes, thought Crystal, there's no doubt she tried to poison me.*

*Crystal suffered from periodic psychosis and the events of the day had escalated her into a psychotic episode.  She had found real love on the island and then fear and hatred within a short time.  Her enemy was trying to kill her and a spirit had been summoned to the boat.*

*Her suspicions of Shelly were heightened when Shelly presented her with another cup of coffee.  She took it out onto the deck and then she spoke softly. 'Hi, Hannah.  I'm really sorry about what we did on your grave. 'They shouldn't have used the Ouija. I'm sorry for that too.'*

*I had heard her words and although disturbed, I decided to take a light approach.*

*'Talking to yourself?'*

*'Oh no, I was talking to Hannah.  She came tonight. You scared her away.'*

*'Hannah?  What are you saying, Crystal?'*

*'Hannah Edwards came to me through the Ouija.*

*I told her I was so sorry we had desecrated her grave. She said it was okay and that she would see me very soon.'*

'Crystal, you didn't see Hannah. I think you should get some sleep. We'll talk about all this in the morning.' I put my arm around her. She tipped her coffee into the river and walked back inside. People were getting ready for bed. Rick had already left the group.

Crystal entered the cabin and pulled the curtain closed. She moved to the bed and whispered in Rick's ear. 'Rick, I'm so afraid. Shelly Lawson is really Rachael Livingstone. She tried to poison me tonight and she's been signalling that big cruiser that's been following us.'

Bradshaw had lived with Crystal and her delusions for five years. What he was hearing was pure fantasy. 'Did you take your medication this morning, Crystal?'

'It's not a delusion Rick. It's true. You've got to believe me.'

'Come to bed. It'll be all better in the morning.'

Crystal was aghast when after listening to her story, Rick just turned over and fell asleep. She felt angry and afraid. She decided to record everything in her diary. If Shelly killed her, then at least it would be all there and maybe someone would read it. There was no way she would record our lovemaking. That was definitely her private business.

She wrote in detail and then tried to sleep. But the stress and fear she was feeling kept her awake. An hour passed. Tomorrow was a public holiday and her mother didn't have to go to work. Most likely she would be up watching the late-night movie. It wouldn't be too late to phone. Crystal had already told her mother about the signalling. Now she needed to tell her about Rachael. She took her mobile out onto the deck, not knowing that Shelly was up on the flight deck giving Golden Girl the 'all clear'.

Shelly had just finished signalling when she saw Crystal. She crept down the stairs and listened as Crystal talked into her mobile phone.

'I thought you'd be up but I'll leave a message anyhow. I've got to tell someone. Mum, I'm so frightened. I tackled Shelly about the signalling and you'll never believe it—Shelly is Rachael Livingstone! I recognised her voice! She's changed her face; that's why I didn't know her at first. But that voice and those eyes—it's her! I told Rick but he thinks I'm having a delusion. Tonight, she gave me coffee and I'm pretty sure it was poisoned. I didn't drink it. Oh, I know it sounds like paranoia, but it's real. In case something happens to me, I'll record all this in my diary. If all goes well, I'll be reporting it all to the police when we anchor in the morning. Knowing Rachael, drugs are involved. I'll call you tomorrow.' She flipped the phone closed, and that was the last thing that happened in Crystal's life. Shelly came up behind her and swung the heavy signalling torch down onto her head. Shelly's superior muscle development gave her the strength of a man. Her blow was crushing and deadly.

Lance's dinghy was approaching. He cut the

motor as it neared the boat and took up the oars. As he came alongside, the dinghy bumped against the boat.

'Come around to the stern,' whispered Shelly. Lance rowed the dinghy to the stern. He saw Crystal lying on the deck. 'Christ, what's happened?'

'She guessed my identity and knows what we're doing. She was going to report it tomorrow. I had to kill her.'

'She's dead?'

'Yeah. She's dead.'

'Well, that's going to cause a major problem.'

'You'll have to get rid of her. Dump her out to sea.'

'Why not the river?'

'Don't be daft. Dozens of boats go up and down this river every minute of every day. She'd be found in no time. Take her to Golden Girl and then dump her out to sea on your way back to the marina. Make sure you weigh her down.'

Together they bundled Crystal onto the dinghy and Gibson gave Shelly a duffle bag. He rowed away trying to avoid looking at the girl lying near his feet. Shelly watched as the dinghy cut quietly through the still water.

Gibson was a drug dealer with low morals, but he didn't like murder. Neither did his crew. He couldn't risk taking Crystal's body aboard Golden Girl. He came alongside the big cruiser, boarded, picked up a shovel and motored out to the little nearby island. He dragged Crystal's body ashore and started digging.

Lance Gibson had been leading a soft life these past ten years and he was totally unfit. Digging in that *heavy, gritty sand was not easy. As he shovelled the sand over Crystal, he noticed the bright green bracelet. The stones looked too flashy and too gaudy to be real emeralds. He decided it was just cheap costume jewellery and continued to shovel. It wasn't long before he'd had enough. If he continued digging, he reckoned he'd have a heart attack. Anyway, no one came to this little plot. It would be fine.*

*On the boat, Shelly emptied the duffle bag. There were eight packages containing a pure white powder. She placed each packet into the eight pockets she had made in the underside of the caftan's skirt. She picked up Crystal's mobile, turned it off and put it in one of the pockets. She then checked the deck for bloodstains and untied the dinghy. She hoped the empty dinghy would suggest that Crystal had drowned in the river. The anticipated, easy landing of the drugs on this pleasure cruise was turning into a big, ugly nightmare. She went inside and, after a long while, fell asleep.*

*Shelly woke to the sound of raised voices. She walked out onto the deck just as I dived into the river. Then Rick flashed past and dived in too. This was her chance. She had to get hold of Crystal's diary.*

*She went to the cabin and found Crystal's bag. The diary was there. On the inside front cover was written: 'Gabrielle Chambers (Mum), Flat 4, 26 Beauchamp Street, Dulwich Hill. Shelly put that in her memory bank and turned to the last entry. Sure enough, it was all there—the signalling between the two boats and Crystal's suspicions that drugs were involved. Then Crystal's damning accusation: Shelly is really Rachael*

Livingstone. She tried to poison me tonight. I think she will try again.

'What are you doing here?' Rick was standing in the doorway, dripping water.

'I thought something might be in Crystal's diary, something that might help us find her.'

'And is there?'

'She wrote that she and Brett had sex on the island yesterday.'

'That's crap. Give me that!' Rick snatched the diary and started rifling through the pages.

'It's true. I saw them. I followed them up the track. There were some graves up the top. He screwed her on a grave.'

Rick felt a thudding in his head. He hadn't missed the looks that had passed between Crystal and me. He knew there was a strong attraction, but he had told himself it would come to nothing. Now Shelly's words hit him like bullets. He slammed the book shut and glared at her.

'Crystal also wrote that if you found out, you would kill her. You have to get rid of that diary, Rick. Everyone knew about the diary. Someone will tell the police and when they read it, you'll be the prime suspect.' Shelly hoped her quick-thinking lies would propel Rick to destroy the diary.

'You're talking like she's dead.'

'She couldn't swim. She must have drowned. The coast guard will be here any minute. You've got to throw it overboard.'

They heard Danni's voice from the deck. 'Brett,

*the dinghy's missing. Crystal's gone off in the dinghy.'*

*Rick grinned. 'Hear that? Crystal's gone off in the dinghy. She's alive.' He slid the diary beneath the belt on his shorts. 'I'm not throwing her diary anywhere.' He stumbled up the stairs and ran out onto the deck. Shelly followed.*

*When I heard Danni's voice, I swam back to the boat. The missing dinghy had given me hope. Maybe Crystal had drifted down the river and couldn't get back. Rick and Shelly were standing near the stairs. As I passed them, Rick grabbed my arm. He was raging like a mad bull. 'You're responsible for this you fuckwit. I know what you did on the island. It's all in her diary. You fucked her on a bloody grave.' His words stunned me. I pushed him off and climbed up to the flight deck.*

*A loud thudding noise in the distance gradually increased to deafening proportions. The marine rescue helicopter came into view. It hovered overhead for a few minutes and then swept away. Soon after, the powerful marine rescue launch came into view. It pulled alongside and two men hopped on board. One of the men was shouting over the din of the helicopter. 'We found a dinghy downstream—empty.' These words had a chilling effect on all of us. Another launch approached, towing the dinghy. It dropped three divers into the murky river at various points. The two men climbed up to the flight deck.*

*Shelly motioned to Rick and they entered the main cabin. 'You've got to throw the diary. Crystal's dead. You'll be accused.'*

*Rick went out on the deck and threw the book as*

far as he could. It floated for a few seconds and then slowly slipped from view. Shelly drew in a sigh of relief. Neither of them was aware of a pair of eyes watching from the flight deck.

Soon after, Marine Rescue gave instructions for us to return to shore.

\*

Back in our apartment Shelly changed her clothes and threw the caftan into a suitcase. She then packed as many clothes, shoes and cosmetics as she could fit in. She pulled her briefcase out of the cupboard and packed in her laptop and personal papers. She put a fake police ID in her pocket and slammed out of the apartment. In the downstairs garage, she selected a hammer from my toolbox, slipped it into the briefcase, and headed across Sydney to the apartment in Dulwich Hill.

\*

Gabrielle Chambers had woken around eight that morning. She welcomed the holiday but was worried about Crystal. She took her coffee out onto her small deck and enjoyed the sunlight on her face. It was a real treat to be able to relax and not have to rush to the factory. But her joy was marred by her fears. Crystal's recent phone calls were a worry. Were they real or were they a figment of her imagination? This beautiful daughter had recently come back into her life. This child she had had to abandon when she herself was a child, was now her reason for living. She had been troubled when she discovered Crystal's mental problems but quickly decided she would give her all the love and *security necessary to banish this illness. They would make up for lost time and have a wonderful future.*

*Gabrielle left her deck, deciding she would try phoning Crystal's mobile. She was surprised to see her answering machine flashing. Crystal's message alarmed her. She called Crystal's mobile but it was turned off. Should she call the police? If so, what would she say? Crystal had a history of mental illness and the message sounded like the delusion of a mentally unstable mind. Maybe it was a delusion. Gabrielle decided to wait. She tried Crystal's mobile again at ten. It was still turned off. She called the marina but the boat hadn't berthed.*

*Three hours later she opened the door to a tall young woman who flashed a police badge.*

*'Mrs Chambers?'*

*'Ms Chambers, actually,' said Gabrielle.*

*'I'm Detective Sergeant Ruth Farrell. May I come in?'*

*'Is it about Crystal?'*

*'Yes.' Shelly entered the flat and looked around. Gabrielle closed the door.*

*'What's happened?'*

*'I'm afraid Crystal's gone missing.'*

*'Oh no! Where?' Gabrielle felt a tight band wrap around her gut. She had lost Crystal once. She couldn't face losing her again.*

*'She disappeared last night. Did she contact you?'*

*'Yes, but I was asleep. She left a message. Do you want to hear it?'*

*'Yes.'*

Gabrielle replayed the message.  Although Shelly had heard it the previous night, she listened as if she was hearing it for the first time.

'Have you mentioned this message to anyone else?'

'No.  I was waiting to hear from Crystal.'

'Are you sure you haven't told anyone?'

'Of course, I'm sure.'

'I would like to see anything you might have that's connected with Crystal.'

'She doesn't live here.  All I have are newspaper articles and some letters.'

'May I see them?'

Gabrielle had kept the articles and letters from Crystal in a file in her bedroom drawer.  She handed them to Shelly who asked, 'May I take them?'

'They are very precious to me.  You will return them?'

'Of course.  I'll make copies and bring them here myself this time tomorrow.

Thanks, Ms Chambers.  I'm sure Crystal will turn up okay.  Could I trouble you for a glass of water?'

Gabrielle went into the kitchen.  Shelly zipped open her briefcase, withdrew the hammer, and followed Gabrielle quietly.  As Gabrielle filled a glass with water, Shelly delivered a crushing, lethal blow to her head. She checked Gabrielle's pulse and then dragged the lifeless body to the bathroom.

She arranged Gabrielle's head against the sharp tiled shower hob, sprinkled water on the floor, and splashed some on Gabrielle's shoes.  It had to look like

*an accident. She checked for bloodstains, grabbed
the message tape, and left the apartment with the door
still locked on the inside.*

Yes, it was all there. Now that I know exactly or
near exactly what happened, I felt a sense of relief and
a feeling that at last, I might find closure.

The next day, Ben, Danni, Steve and Jaz called
to see me. They listened in disbelief as I told them the
full story. 'You didn't believe Crystal was dead, did you
Brett?' asked Danni.
'I probably didn't want to.'
'You put a lot of store on the bracelet.'
'I'd never seen it on her,' I said.
'I've been thinking about that. It was a very
expensive piece of jewellery. All those stones were real
emeralds. I think Crystal decided not to wear it during
the day in case she lost it. I can only remember seeing
her wear it on the last night,' recalled Danni.
'I'm sure you're right. I did put too much store on
the bracelet.'
'Well, what now, mate?' asked Steve playfully
ruffling my hair.
'As soon as I get out of here, I'll be heading back
home.'
'This time, you're not going to disappear on us.
Give us your address,' Danni said.
After they left, I lay my head back on my propped-
up pillow, feeling warm and peaceful. My room was three
floors up and my window overlooked a big circular park.

Autumn had arrived and lush green leaves were already mottled with shades of gold and amber as the trees entered the third stage of their annual life cycle. I watched the people in the park and thought about the life cycle of humans. Some cycles continue for nearly one hundred years; others, like Crystal's, are cut off in early summer. She never would see autumn or winter. She would never grow old. I smiled as I watched the children playing games and the young adults jogging or cycling. The autumn people strolled quietly, often with a dog on a leash. Then there were the winter people, some leaning on canes, others shuffling along, all happy to have a place in the sun.

I felt a great peace descend on me. At that moment, I knew that I had loved Crystal. She had given me moments of joy and happiness that rarely come along. Grieving for her had set me on a healing path. Now that her killer had suffered the greatest retribution, I could at last find total closure. I could start again. I felt an incredible weight lift from me and I was seized with yet another bout of pure happiness.

I then became aware of a presence in the room. Crystal was standing in the doorway. She walked toward me. I was seized by joy and fear. Maybe I had died and Crystal was welcoming me into the afterlife. Then I realised it wasn't Crystal. This was not an apparition. It was Cleo. She came to the bed and sat on the edge. Her eyes were full of tears. 'I just heard the news. How are you?' she whispered.

'I'm okay. I'll be out soon.' I said, feeling a rush of relief to know I was still alive. Cleo started sobbing.

'Hey'. I touched her arm with one of my bandaged hands. 'Don't cry. I'm okay.'

'I'm crying with gladness. I thought you might have been a lot worse.' She softly touched one of my hands. 'Do they hurt much?'

'They give me stuff for the pain. It's fine.'

Cleo kicked off her shoes and lay next to me on the bed. She put her head on my shoulder. I enjoyed the warmth of her closeness and her apple-blossom fragrance. 'What will you do when you leave here?'

'As soon as I can drive, I'll be heading home.'

'Port Stephens?'

'Yes.' We lay quietly for a few moments and then she raised herself on one elbow and gazed steadily into my eyes.

'Port Stephens is a lovely place?'

'Yes.'

'The people are nice?'

'Yes.'

'The beaches are beautiful?'

'Yes.'

'The climate's good?'

'Yes.'

'I want you to really consider your answer to the next question.'

'Go on.'

'Do they need a good interior decorator up there?'

'Yes.' I shouted.

We both laughed and then she kissed me.

crystal

www.ingramcontent.com/pod-product-compliance
Lightning Source LLC
Chambersburg PA
CBHW021859020426
42334CB00013B/403